"I can't think of anything better tha  of his wilderness. Zeke Pipher k a practical guide filled with wisd is the kind of guy I'd hang out with in the woods and lone church—a rare combination. If you want to worship God like a man, this is a great resource!"

—**Rick Johnson**, bestselling author of *A Man in the Making* and *The Power of a Man*

"God put within man the desire to create, to build, to accomplish— to be a man! We honor and worship the Father when we do these things according to the Scriptures and the guidance of his Holy Spirit. We represent the Father in our pursuits every day, just like an earthly son represents his father. We can make our Father proud or we can bring dishonor to his name. Today it's harder than ever to go out into the world and make him proud. *In Pursuit* is a relevant and valuable tool to remind me daily just who it is I am trying to emulate as I create, build, and accomplish."

—**James Brion**, TV producer, host, and outfitter

"I grew up a hunter, not a Christian, but the woods and fields taught me to be still and quiet, and that is the ideal state for God to reach in and tap us on the shoulder—and then touch our lives. Though I have been a Christian for thirty years now, being in the field still creates the perfect opportunity for reflection and renewal. Zeke Pipher obviously knows this very well, as his book clearly illustrates the unique relationship outdoorsmen have with their Creator. In this collection of short stories with big lessons, Zeke uses simple times in the woods to speak to issues of life and Christian maturity. It is first and foremost a book about devotion, but it sure is fun to find those lessons packaged in a format I can identify with so well. I would recommend this book to any outdoorsman."

—**Bill Winke**, outdoor writer and host of *Midwest Whitetail* TV

"Zeke Pipher has spent his life exploring creation. He has followed the call on his life to learn and guide others to the Creator. Zeke shares what he's experienced and learned about creation and the

Creator with this book. I truly enjoyed reading it and will share the devotionals with others. Everyone who enjoys wild critters and places will enjoy and benefit from *In Pursuit.*

—**Dr. Grant Woods,** wildlife biologist
and host of www.GrowingDeer.tv

"Zeke Pipher writes with strength and clarity about who we are and who God is, and he does so in the setting of the beautiful and rugged creation that surrounds us. In story after story and insight after insight—all offered up in a quick, easy-to-read style—Pipher takes us on a wilderness journey with God and Scripture to the very heart of what matters most in our lives and our world. There's something for everyone here. A great book."

—**Murray Pura,** pastor and author of *Rooted, Streams,*
and *Majestic and Wild*

"*In Pursuit* is an amazing ministry. Zeke does a masterful job of combining his love of the great outdoors and fascinating wildlife experiences with his theological expertise. The result is a perfect spiritual experience for the hunter or fisherman."

—**Andy Hoffman,** father of 2013 ESPY winner Jack Hoffman
and chairman of the Team Jack Foundation

In Pursuit

IN PURSUIT

DEVOTIONS FOR THE HUNTER AND FISHERMAN

ZEKE PIPHER

BakerBooks

a division of Baker Publishing Group
Grand Rapids, Michigan

© 2014 by Ezekiel Pipher

Published by Baker Books
a division of Baker Publishing Group
P.O. Box 6287, Grand Rapids, MI 49516-6287
www.bakerbooks.com

Printed in the United States of America

Library of Congress Cataloging-in-Publication Data is on file at the Library of Congress, Washington, DC.

ISBN 978-0-8010-1586-1 (pbk.)

Published in association with the Books & Such Literary Agency.

14   15   16   17   18   19   20   7   6   5   4   3   2   1

For Kate, Aidan, and Claire

CONTENTS

FOREWORD

Several years ago I realized that the only thing better than going out into creation and enjoying all that it has to offer is letting the Creator come into me and enjoying all he has to offer. This change in my frame of mind as an outdoorsman completely altered the way I entered the fields and woods.

Before this discovery my only focus as I hunted was the challenge of outsmarting the amazingly well-developed defensive skills of animals like deer and elk, as well as birds like the wild turkey. After I understood that God, my Maker, wanted to use my love of his creation as an entry door into my soul, I began actively and deliberately looking for the ways he would do it. The first time I saw how God could use the outdoors to change my inner man took place just after dawn one frosty morning while I was sitting on a deer stand.

As I sat hoping for the appearance of a whitetail, the sun began to send its bright streams of light through the timber. One of the rays seemed to fall on me like a theater spotlight, and that's when I noticed that as I exhaled, a thick white mist was boiling out of my mouth forming a floating cloud in front of my face. The wind was calm that morning so the puff just hung there for a few seconds, then drifted slowly away. I assumed that in the sunlight, the movement of the mist was something that could be easily seen by the keen eyes of a deer, so I attempted a few things to stop it.

I tried exhaling slower, then faster, out of the side of my mouth, and even into my gloves. Nothing worked. The clouds still formed and tumbled noticeably in the sunlit air. Finally, I gave up on my efforts to conceal the evidence that I was a breathing being and started playing with the fog I couldn't stop.

I tried making rings with it the way I've seen people do with cigars. I looked skyward and pretended I was an Indian sending smoke signals. And at one point I smiled as the thought of breakfast made me wonder if I could create the shape of a plate of biscuits and gravy. Then, a few moments later, something surprisingly serious happened. As another white cloud of my breath wafted off into the woods, a familiar verse from the book of James drifted into my mind: "You are just a vapor that appears for a little while and then vanishes away" (4:14 NASB).

I began to see myself in the temporary clouds I was making. As each one appeared then disappeared, I quietly thought, *That's me, that's Annie (my wife), that's my children, that's life!*

To have an encounter with such a profound and undeniable truth while on a deer stand actually caught me a little off guard. I never expected that my emotions could turn all mushy and reflective while I was engaged in the rawness of a hunt. Yet they did. Even though it felt a little awkward and unusual, it felt good . . . and it felt right.

I left the woods that day a different man. Understanding that the "hang time" of my own vapor of life was not all that long, the changes that came were real and lasting. From showing my family more attention to embracing friendships a little tighter to being more mindful of my spiritual health, I felt motivated to make sure my cloud counted for something good.

After that unforgettable epiphany, I started looking for other eternal truths that God wanted me to "harvest" while enjoying his great outdoors. There have been many, and most of those insights have been written into several books to help other outdoorsmen see them as well.

Because there seems to be a growing hunger among hunters and anglers for books that feed their souls, and because I'm well aware that I can't reach every one of them with my own writing, I was doubly excited to know that Zeke Pipher had chosen to put his own discoveries into a book. *In Pursuit* is skillfully written and is full of well-told stories to illustrate the biblical truths he presents.

Whether you've been a follower of Christ for a long time or you're new to the "narrow trail," you'll be glad you have a copy of this book because on every page you'll find directions that will help guide you to higher spiritual ground.

Steve Chapman
Author, *A Look at Life from a Deer Stand*
www.steveandanniechapman.com

Acknowledgments

I would like to express my appreciation of my friends who enjoy the great outdoors with me—Chris Blaine, Jeff Brehm, Darrin Brumbaugh, Bryan Clark, R. B. and Bev Drickey, Philip Esslinger, Matt Green, Jason Hince, Thom Ludtke, Matt Mahar, Tom Osborne, Scott Ratliff, Michael Strauser, Brodie Swisher, Mike Toukan, and Scott Westlund. I also want to express my respect for Charlie Alsheimer, Joe Bell, Christian Berg, Steve Chapman, and Dan Schmidt—I value their friendship as well as their excellent work as writers, photographers, and editors in the outdoor world.

Thanks to my readers and editors—Bryan Clark, Scott Johnson, Linda Peterson, Jamie Pipher, Mary Pipher, J. J. Springer, and Jon Wilcox. Thanks also to my colleagues at Heartland EFC—Dan Bailey, Brandon Hamer, Mike Husman, Scott Johnson, Mark McHargue, Nathan Musgrave, and J. J. Springer. It is a privilege and pleasure to serve alongside these elders and pastors. They give me time to write, interact with my ideas, and regularly stir me up to love and good works.

Finally, I am deeply grateful for the four people I most enjoy "going outside" with—my wife, Jamie, and our three children, Kate, Aidan, and Claire. In addition to spending time in nature with me, they have generously given me time to fish and hunt and collect the stories contained in this book.

Note to the Reader

Five years ago, a seasoned elk guide called me and said, "If you'll meet me in New Mexico, I'll teach you how to hunt elk." I had never hunted elk before, and the one time I had tried to make a bugle on an elk call, I sounded like a donkey caught in a foot trap. I took my friend up on his offer, and for seven days he taught me how to read elk sign, dialogue with bulls, and scamper up and down mountains to get into position. I went into the trip as green as the pine trees we napped under, but I walked away an elk hunter. The secret to my evolution: I listened to my guide's voice.

The book of Proverbs presents wisdom as a person, a guide, who calls out to us and offers to teach us how to live. "Wisdom cries aloud in the street, in the markets she raises her voice" (Prov. 1:20). The promise Wisdom makes to us is that if we will listen to her voice and put her words into action, she will help us live a life rich in meaning, purpose, and relationship with God. "Whoever listens to me will dwell secure and will be at ease, without dread of disaster" (Prov. 1:33).

I wrote *In Pursuit* to help sportsmen listen to Wisdom's voice through God's Word. It's meant to be a companion book to the Bible, not a replacement of the Scriptures. If you only have time to read one or the other, feed your soul from the choicest meat, the Bible. Yet, if you have time for both, *In Pursuit* will illustrate, explain, and apply truth in ways that will help you better understand God's Word. To make the most of this book, I would suggest reading the passage referenced at the beginning of each devotion. I carefully selected passages that are relevant to the content and that will help you interact with Wisdom's voice on a deeper level. The prayers at the end of each devotion are simply to "prime the pump" and lead you into a personal conversation with God about your life.

I'm thankful to the men and women who let me tell their stories in this book—I have changed many of their names and a few of the minor details in order to protect their identities. Many of the ideas and illustrations in this devotional came to me while I was sitting in tree stands along the Platte River in Nebraska or fly-fishing in one of Colorado's many trout streams. I tried to bring these moments in nature into my writing in such a way that, with every flip of a page, you would smell hints of Nebraska cedar or hear the rumbling of a Colorado stream. My hope for you is that as you read *In Pursuit*, you will sense the nearness of God, the friendship of the author, and the exhilaration of creation. Enjoy the pursuit, my friend.

IN PURSUIT

DEVOTIONS FOR THE
HUNTER AND FISHERMAN

1

THE GIGANTIC SECRET

Scripture Passage: *"Behold, the dwelling place of God is with man. He will dwell with them, and they will be his people, and God himself will be with them as their God."* —Revelation 21:3

READ: GENESIS 2

We often want the good things God gives but not God himself. When we do this, we act like my German wirehair when he wants a bone. Ezra has the uncanny ability to sense when I've visited the pet store. I'll pull into the driveway, and he'll be sitting obediently in his kennel with eager eyes and a wagging tail. When I let him out, he treats me like I'm a god, performing tricks, licking my hand, and rubbing up against my hip as if to say, "You're the most important thing in my world." And then I give him the bone, and he takes it to the corner of the garage, wraps his slobbery gums around it, and gives me a look as if to say, "Stay away. If you try to take my bone, I'll bite your hand off!"

We are the ones who lose out when we have this attitude toward God. We weren't made to enjoy life apart from our Creator. The book of Genesis shows us a major design feature about us as people: we were meant to find our significance, pleasure, and acceptance in a close relationship with our Maker. God created us to be with him. The Garden of Eden was paradise, not primarily because the fruit was luscious and the lions were friendly, but because God was so close to Adam and Eve. God's voice was the sound of warmth, pleasure, and familiarity to them. His presence provided this first couple with unending excitement and challenge.

We are all created to need this closeness to God. When we act like my dog, trying to enjoy God's gifts apart from God, it leaves us unsatisfied. Some of the most miserable people in the world have fancy homes, big families, and gigantic tracts of land. Yet, they still feel empty inside because they are trying to enjoy these things without Jesus. Nothing God gives us, no matter how good the gift, holds the power to satisfy us like his presence. As Psalm 17:15 states, "As for me, I shall behold your face in righteousness; when I awake, I shall be satisfied with your likeness."

Thanks to the gospel of Jesus Christ, we can be rightly related to God and experience his presence and pleasure every moment of every day. We don't need to take the meaty, delicious bones that God gives us and then run off to a dark, private place, growling at the Giver if he makes a move in our direction. We get to do life with him, experiencing a joy that's unfamiliar to those who don't know him. As G. K. Chesterton said, "Joy, which was the small publicity of the pagan, is the gigantic secret of the Christian."[1]

Are you experiencing the gigantic secret of the Christian life? You can be—all you need to do is choose to live life with God by grace through faith in his Son.

Prayer

God, you have created me to know you in a personal way. Help me to not be merely religious, practicing rituals and making sacrifices without engaging my heart. Help me keep you the most important thing in my life, even more important than your amazing gifts. Amen.

1. G. K. Chesterton, *Orthodoxy*, vol. 1 of *G. K. Chesterton Collected Works* (San Francisco: Ignatius Press, 1986), 365.

2

ALWAYS IN PURSUIT

Scripture Passage: *"So we are always of good courage.*
We know that while we are at home in the body we are
away from the Lord, for we walk by faith, not by sight."
—2 Corinthians 5:6–7

READ: HEBREWS 11

I clean my hunting room once a year, usually in January, after deer season. By the middle of winter, not even Christopher Columbus would be able to discover the floor of that room in our basement—it's mounded to the ceiling with dirty clothes, empty hand warmer packages, and hunting gear.

A few years ago, my ten-year-old son, Aidan, joined me in the annual cleaning ritual. As we were rummaging through what remained from last season's hunting expeditions, he found a green slip of paper. "What's this, Dad?"

"That's the unfilled tag from my Kansas deer hunt," I replied.

A few moments later he asked, "What about this one?"

"That's from my elk hunt to Oregon, bud."

"And this one?" he asked, holding up yet another piece of paper.

I wanted to say, "Let's stop talking and get back to work," but I swallowed hard, and replied, "Uh, well . . . that's my turkey tag from Nebraska."

He looked at the three tags, paused for a moment, and then exclaimed, "Wow, you did a lot of hunting this season, but not a lot of catching."

Every sportsman knows the experience of pursuing something that he can't quite catch. This reminds me of the Christian life this side of eternity. We are ever in pursuit of God—wanting to see Jesus, hear his voice, and witness his every move. And while we have his Spirit with us at all times, we know that we will not be with him until we are in glory. This physical separation from the one we love the most creates a longing in us. The apostle Paul phrased this perfectly when he said, "We would rather be away from the body and at home with the Lord" (2 Cor. 5:8). So in this life we wait. And while we wait, we keep pursuing.

There are several parallels between the life of a sportsman and the life of a Christian. Both require a thoughtful, diligent, patient approach. As the sportsman spends hours studying his terrain, checking his equipment, and preparing for the moment he encounters his prey, so the Christian also prepares himself to meet God. This involves pursuing a God who we cannot see yet. It also means learning about God through reading the Scriptures, talking with God by praying, and developing greater discipline to obey God's commands. There is no shortcut to successfully pursuing God; it takes great commitment and diligence. Again, Paul says it well: "I press on toward the goal for the prize of the upward call of God in Christ Jesus" (Phil. 3:14).

Being with Jesus in heaven one day will make all the work worthwhile.

Abraham Lincoln once said, "With the catching ends the pleasure of the chase." The opposite is true of the Christian life, for the moment we actually "catch" God—stand in Jesus's presence and apprehend his beauty and power—will be the *beginning* of paradise. For the Christian, when the chase ends, true life begins.

Prayer

Jesus, I can't wait to actually see you face-to-face. Please give me the strength and courage of heart to pursue you until that moment. Help me have no other interests that take priority over my passion to know you and be changed into your image. Amen.

3

RUGGED, EMPTY INDIVIDUALISM

Scripture Passage: *"Rather, speaking the truth in love,*
we are to grow up in every way into him who is the head,
into Christ, from whom the whole body, joined and held
together by every joint with which it is equipped, when
each part is working properly, makes the body grow so
that it builds itself up in love." —Ephesians 4:15–16

READ: 1 CORINTHIANS 12:12–26

"I don't need organized religion! I spend time with God in the great outdoors. The woods are my sanctuary!"

A man in elk camp lifted both of his arms in the air, looked up at the canyons surrounding our campfire, and made that declaration in response to my question, "Where do you go to church?" Three other men in camp affirmed their agreement to his statement of rugged individualism.

This attitude is both true and false. On one hand, every sportsman should worship God in his creation. That's one of the primary reasons why God gave us nature—he wanted us to see his power and character in the breathtaking things he's created. "For what can be known about God is plain to them, because God has shown it to them. For his invisible attributes, namely, his eternal power and divine nature, have been clearly perceived, ever since the creation of the world, in the things that have been made" (Rom. 1:19–20).

For a person who follows Jesus, all of life is holy. Every place we find ourselves is a sacred space—forests, fields, living rooms, garages, and sanctuaries. We are with God in all of these places. But not all spaces inspire the same response from us. Like many reading this book, I sense a special connection with my Creator when I'm surrounded by trees or when I'm on the water—far from concrete, cars, and other things made with human hands. It is entirely appropriate to worship in nature.

But if an attitude of rugged individualism prevents us from holding a deep commitment to our local community of believers, we lose something special. And when we are absent from our spiritual community, we cause others to lose something special as well. The apostle Paul describes our choice to put our faith in Jesus as an immersion by the Spirit of God into the body of Christ (cf. 1 Cor. 12:13). When we gain salvation, we are no longer isolated, autonomous beings; we become vital, interdependent members of a unified community. As Paul states, "Now you are the body of Christ and individually members of it" (1 Cor. 12:27).

One of the most ruggedly independent, courageous steps a sportsman can take today is to turn away from his previously isolated life and say, "I'm going to do the difficult work of committing deeply to my local church. I'm going to be a man who serves others and allows myself to be served by others. I'm going to play my role in the body."

When a man does this, he gains not only the beauty of worshiping God by himself in creation but also the thrill of being shoulder to shoulder with his brothers and sisters in Christ. As satisfying as it is to spend time in nature, nothing can replace the adventure we embarked on when the Spirit of God baptized us into the body of Christ. We were once alone, but no more. We are now a part of the greatest community on earth.

Prayer

Holy Spirit, thank you for baptizing me into the body of Christ at the moment of my salvation. Now please give me the commitment of heart to participate and contribute to my local church. Help me lay down my sense of rugged, empty individualism for a sense of community. Amen.

4

Deep Wisdom

Scripture Passage: *"How much better to get wisdom than gold! To get understanding is to be chosen rather than silver."* —Proverbs 16:16

Read: Proverbs 1

"Don't move, Aidan. Turkeys have phenomenal sight and you'll spook them," RB whispered to Aidan, my ten-year-old son. Aidan stood completely motionless, his forehead just a few inches away from the mesh window on the side of the ground blind. A flock of turkeys had moseyed over the hill and into our setup. Four large toms were puffed up and fanned out just ten feet from Aidan's pancake-sized eyes.

RB taught me to turkey hunt nineteen years ago, when I was just a nervous young man dating his daughter. He drove me out to a stretch of timber along the Niobrara River in northern Nebraska and called in a twenty-one-pound Merriam's gobbler for me. Now, just a few miles away from that spot along the river, I watched that great man pass on the same wisdom to his ten-year-old grandson.

The more old and young connect with each other, the better it is for both generations. Sadly, our society works against this important goal. We tend to push the older generations to the periphery, perhaps paying lip service to their importance, but then asking them to stay out of the way. We also isolate our children from the world of adults, encouraging them to spend most of their time with peers. This is tragic because there is a deep and time-tested knowledge that resides within older men who walk with Jesus.

The book of Proverbs tells us that wisdom and knowledge are more valuable than anything else in the world. If this is indeed true, then we ought to pursue spiritual growth and maturity with more passion and fervor than we do earning money, establishing a reputation, or building a successful career. In this pursuit, the older and wiser among us are invaluable.

Let me encourage you to seek out an older, wiser man to sit under and learn from. Because this culture has convinced many older saints that they have little to offer, you may need to begin your relationship by convincing your spiritual mentor that his input is valuable to you. And it is. I've learned much of how to be a husband, father, and friend from men who have walked with Jesus for twenty, forty, and even sixty years. These men know God's Word, have experienced God's grace, and have sensed the power of God's Spirit helping them. I'm a pastor, author, and speaker today largely because I've had wise, humble, God-fearing men build into my life for the past twenty-five years. I wish the same for you.

Prayer

Father, help me remain teachable to older, wiser men who have walked with you faithfully for years. Please help me to ask good questions, listen well, and put into practice the truth they teach and model. Thank you for these men you have brought into my life. Amen.

5

HUNT LOVE

Scripture Passage: *"This is my commandment, that you love one another as I have loved you."*—John 15:12

READ: 1 CORINTHIANS 13:1–14:1

Sportsmen are well positioned to understand one of the most essential commands of Christianity: the command to "hunt love." That phrase comes directly from Scripture. Immediately following 1 Corinthians 13—the chapter that defines biblical love—the apostle Paul uses sportsman language to tell us to put this love into action. The first word in 1 Corinthians 14, "pursue," is the Greek word for "hunt," so a literal translation of that command is "hunt love."

I recently returned from an elk hunt in New Mexico. For seven days I hiked up and down the Sangre de Cristo Mountains in sweltering weather, screaming out locator bugles and listening for a reply. In seven days, I never heard an elk answer. Yet I hunted hard, from sunup the first day until sundown the last, because I was zealous about the chase.

"Love" is an easy word to throw around today, but there is nothing easy about actually loving other people the way God commands. To love someone is to maintain an unconditional commitment to meeting their needs above your own. Jesus was the perfect embodiment and definition of this idea. First John 3:16 says, "By this we know love, that he laid down his life for us, and we ought to lay down our lives for the brothers."

Jesus loved by remaining committed to other people's spiritual and physical welfare. Sometimes people turned toward Jesus, accepting his love. However, many of the people Jesus pursued fought him or pushed him aside. They mocked him, ignored him, or attempted to kill him. The work of loving other people, even his enemies, was hard, challenging work, but Jesus stuck with it. We could say he "hunted" it.

Loving other people would be easier if everyone we knew was clean, kind, and full of compliments. But this is not how we would describe the people in our lives, even our family members, closest friends, and neighbors. If we're being honest, we would admit that it's not even how we'd describe ourselves. Hunting love is difficult because *we are difficult.* We're self-centered, greedy, moody people, and when we interact with one another, conflict often arises. This conflict makes us want to take the *easy* path—protecting self and focusing on what others can do for us in order to make our lives better. When we take this easy path and someone becomes difficult, we pull away—if our priority is to see what other people can do for us. When they stop doing, we stop caring. That's the easy path. And Jesus didn't take it.

Jesus hunted down opportunities to love the most unlovable people in his life. He forgave and restored Saul, one of the worst persecutors of the early church. He washed Judas's feet, just hours before Judas would betray him with a kiss. And he prayed for the Roman soldiers while they were in the process of crucifying him. Jesus didn't take the easy path—he helped and served those who were trying to hurt him.

Sportsmen know the work, effort, and commitment required to find success in the field. As men of God, we should take that same attitude of determination into our relationships with even the most unlovable people we encounter. Brothers, with Jesus as our Exemplar, let us never give up the hunt.

Prayer

Father, help me to love others with this same quality of love. Give me a heart that is able to serve not only the "easy" people in my life but those who treat me poorly. I desire to "hunt love," no matter how big the challenge. Amen.

6

THREE TRAILS

Scripture Passage: *"The thief comes only to steal and kill and destroy. I came that they may have life and have it abundantly."* —John 10:10

READ: PSALM 51

It's embarrassing to admit, but I once got lost in the woods by our house, a forest I know like the back of my hand. The sun was setting and I was following a game trail as it meandered through the cedar and cottonwood trees along the river. I was walking with my head down, looking for shed antlers and tracks, when I arrived at a fork in the path that turned into three different trails. The ground looked like a turkey foot, and I was standing in the center needing to choose which toe to follow. I took the middle trail, which proved to be the wrong one. Thirty minutes later, I was in the dark, five hundred yards away from my pickup, completely lost.

When it comes to our orientation to God, there are three different paths from which we can choose.

The first path can be termed *Irreligious*, living our lives as if there is no God. The irreligious believe that they are in control of their own destinies and that they answer to nobody, especially God, for their choices.

The second path is that of *Religious and self-righteous*, a stance of believing in the existence of God but not calibrating our lives in complete and utter dependence upon him. The self-righteous trust in their morality, performance, and rituals as a means to satisfy God and to feel good about themselves.

The third path is *Christianity*, or the life of grace. People who live by grace believe in God's existence while also trusting that the life and death of Jesus make us perfectly acceptable to God.

A Christian's sense of self-worth is based on the person of Jesus, not on their performance.

When was the last time you violated one of God's commands? Perhaps you lied or made fun of someone or looked at pornography. After that moment of sin, how did you handle it?

If you're irreligious, you probably tried to ignore your conscience and that inner voice of conviction. If you don't believe in God, your conscience may bother you from time to time, but for no useful reason. A sore conscience doesn't signify that something is wrong between you and your Creator. It doesn't direct you to repentance. It's merely a nuisance, and like all nuisances you will try to find a way to ignore or dismiss it quickly.

If you're religious, you likely thought about God and then confessed your sins. But you probably tried to find something to do in order to feel better about yourself. Perhaps you put a bit more money in the offering, signed up to help with parking lot duty on Sunday, or read a few extra chapters in the Bible. Self-righteous people need to project confidence and assurance, so when they fail, they try extra hard because their sense of self is based on what they do.

However, as a Christian captured by grace, you knew that your choice to sin was wrong, so you confessed it as sin and asked for forgiveness from the one you had sinned against. And because you understand grace, you also *accepted* God's forgiveness and restoration. You didn't then find something to do to feel better about yourself; you set your gaze ahead, humbly dependent upon God and thankful for the righteousness that is yours through faith in Jesus.

These are the three paths, and only one leads to what Jesus describes as "fullness of life" (John 10:10). May you choose more wisely than I did that day by the river.

Prayer

Jesus, I want to know you and walk with you. I don't want to acknowledge you with my lips but deny you with my life. I want you to be the central and supreme passion of my heart. Amen.

7

NEVER RUN DRY

Scripture Passage: *"Whoever drinks of the water that
I will give him will never be thirsty again. The water
that I will give him will become in him a spring of water
welling up to eternal life."* —John 4:14

READ: ISAIAH 55

Jesus spoke these words to a woman who was struggling. She lived
in a time and place not friendly to women. She was a Samaritan,
and the Jews considered Samaritans dirty and substandard. And
she was also a sinner who had failed in marriage five times and now
was living with a sixth man. Life had met this woman in a back
alley, beaten her silly, and left her for dead. When she went to the
well that day, she was needy, exhausted, and dry-mouthed thirsty.

This woman, in many ways, represents us. We all feel the ham-
mering fists of this harsh world at times. We're all painfully aware
of our oddities, weaknesses, and sin. We've all made decisions that
we deeply regret. We're all thirsty, but with a thirst deeper than the
dry-throated, pasty-tongued craving for water. Like this woman,
we crave refreshment for our souls.

We find the refreshment we're longing for in a personal relationship with Jesus. Some people try to make life with God one more
item on their to-do list.

Go to work . . . check.

Mow the lawn . . . check.

Spend time with God . . . check.

As a pastor, people frequently ask me how much time they
should spend reading the Bible or praying. They're looking for an
objective, concrete answer so that they can put it down on paper,

perform it, and then mark it off. God, according to that attitude, is not refreshing. He's not living water to someone thinking religiously. He's only living water to someone thinking relationally.

As Jesus sat with the Samaritan woman, he offered himself as the living water. Not as a religion or a set of rituals. Not as a path to self-righteousness. Not as a set of formulas for making life work. Jesus offered himself—God's presence and grace—to a woman desperately in need of salvation. This is what Jesus still offers us today, for this is what we truly crave and need. When we see Jesus accurately, by the help of the Spirit, we will be drawn to him.

I once camped in an old, abandoned logging camp on Mahogany Mountain in the Owyhee range in eastern Oregon. In the canyon was a plastic pipe wedged between two large boulders. Pure, cold artesian water gushed from the tube. As I spent the day hiking the mountains surrounding the camp, I'd continually return to the waterspout to cup my hands, fill them with water, and drink until I felt refreshed. I didn't go to the well because it was the right thing to do. I didn't drink because someone told me to. I didn't write "Cool throat with fresh water" on a checklist. I sought out the water source and returned to the water source because it was what I desperately needed.

Are you feeling discouraged by life? Are you feeling convicted of sin and tired of the ache of guilt? Does an inner pressure to measure up to God, yourself, or other people wear you out? Perhaps it's time to enjoy the offer from Jesus by trusting in him for your deepest needs. He promises to refresh all who come to him.

"If anyone thirsts, let him come to me and drink. Whoever believes in me, as the Scripture has said, 'Out of his heart will flow rivers of living water'" (John 7:37–38).

There's no need to go through life thirsty. Live by faith in this refreshing Savior and your heart will never run dry again.

Prayer

Father, I am thirsty and I know that only you can provide the water I need. Help me to trust in Jesus as my Savior with all my heart, mind, soul, and strength. I don't want Christianity to be just a religion for me—I want it to be a relationship with you, my loving Father in heaven. Amen.

8

A BUMPER CATCH

Scripture Passage: *"All Scripture is breathed out by God and profitable for teaching, for reproof, for correction, and for training in righteousness, that the man of God may be complete, equipped for every good work."*
—2 Timothy 3:16–17

READ: LUKE 5:1-11

One of the strangest fishing stories ever recorded is found in the Gospel of Luke. Jesus is walking alongside the Sea of Galilee, teaching a crowd about the kingdom of God. People are pressing in on him from all sides. To gain some breathing room, Jesus steps into an empty fishing boat. The owners of the vessel, Simon and Andrew, are standing on the shore cleaning their nets after a slow night of fishing. Jesus asks Simon to push the boat out from shore, they shove off, and Jesus continues to teach the crowd, offshore, about life with God.

Jesus, a carpenter turned rabbi, looks at Simon, a professional fisherman, and says, "Put out into the deep and let down your nets for a catch" (Luke 5:4). Simon was the expert. He was the one who knew everything a fisherman needed to know about the Sea of Galilee. He was the one who had fished his hot spots all night long to no avail. He was the one who knew firsthand, from years of experience, that you don't fish the Sea of Galilee during the day. Simon was the professional, and Jesus had taken command of his ship. You can hear a trace of cynicism as Simon replies, "Master, we toiled all night and took nothing! But at your word I will let down the nets" (Luke 5:5).

Simon is tired and frustrated but willing to go along with Jesus's request. He makes the choice to trust his Master in spite of the previous night's fruitlessness. Moments later, Simon's nets are so full he has to call to other boats and fishermen to help haul in the load. Both Simon's boat and one other boat almost sink because they are so full of fish.

Until that morning, Simon, or Peter, was a full-time fisherman, trying to eke out a living from the sea. And then Jesus stepped onto his boat, told him where to fish, and proved to this fisherman that he was the God of all things, including Simon's fishing career. Now Peter is kneeling before Jesus and calling him "Lord."

As the God of all creation, Jesus has the wisdom and knowledge to lead, teach, and instruct all men in all things, no matter what we do for a living. We may think that a rabbi from the ancient Middle East bears little relevance to our complex, modern lives today, but that couldn't be further from the truth. When Jesus proved to Peter that he governed the sea and all things in it, he demonstrated how he is the God of every aspect of Peter's life, even his career.

In addition to being a pastor, I'm also a freelance outdoor writer and author. As I read the Scriptures each day, I look to Jesus for direction, guidance, and wisdom in all three vocations. When I pray, I ask God for his help, not just for my work at the church, but for each article or book I write. Jesus is my Rabbi—my Teacher and source of wisdom—and I've found that there is no question too difficult for him. There's no vocation beyond his pay grade. And there is no help he can't provide. If you think a bumper catch is something, just wait and see what he'll do in your life as you look to him for help.

Prayer

Jesus, deepen my faith in you and your perfect governance of all things. I trust that you are wise enough to lead me in every area of my life. Help me look to you as I make decisions in my home, work, friendships, and greater community. Amen.

9

CLEARING OUT
THE CLUTTER

Scripture Passage: *"And rising very early in the morning, while it was still dark, he departed and went out to a desolate place, and there he prayed."* —Mark 1:35

READ: PROVERBS 1:2–6

Many people charge so hard through life that they have all but forgotten how to simply enjoy a moment. This has happened to one of my good friends. I've known Ted for several years. As a boy growing up in northern Minnesota, he spent all his free time outside. He spent most afternoons after school and most weekends camping, fishing, and exploring the vast forests just outside his small town. Nobody had to tell Ted how to enjoy nature. As a teenager, he could step onto the floor of his dad's bass boat and do nothing but enjoy the smell of fresh air and the sound of the water slapping against the aluminum hull as he and his dad trolled from one fishing hole to another.

I recently spoke with Ted upon his return from a fishing trip to Canada. I'd been excited for him to get away. He'd been under a lot of stress at work, and it was taking its toll on his body. This man who had once brimmed with youth and health now had to pack prescriptions for high blood pressure and high cholesterol on his trip to Ontario.

When he returned, I asked Ted if he'd been refreshed by nature. He bit his lower lip and shook his head. He had a look of panic on his face as he explained how he couldn't go thirty minutes without fiddling on his smartphone. He called back to the office several times a day to check on clients. While his friends were casting their lines or poking the fire, Ted was reading emails, texts, and Facebook messages. As Ted handed his passport to the customs agent at the border, he realized that he was returning from Canada without having been there.

He had an anxious look on his face as he asked me, "When did I forget how to enjoy life?"

Many men run at a fast clip today, trying to patch together a meaningful life among the demands of work, family, and a myriad of outdoor pursuits. Men's minds are full—and constantly plugged into smartphones, computers, and television—yet many still feel like there's more life to be lived. Could our busy lives be crowding out the deepest experience of life and joy? T. S. Eliot captured the threat when he asked these questions:

Where is the life we have lost in living?
Where is the wisdom we have lost in knowledge?
Where is the knowledge we have lost in information?[1]

Men need to clear out the clutter of competing information in order to sit down, take a deep breath, read the Scriptures, and pray to their Father in heaven. This might mean taking a Bible to the tree stand or the bass boat for some uninterrupted reading. It could mean spending time in prayer in the cab of your truck over the lunch hour, or in the quietness of the morning before other people wake up. We were created to reflect on the goodness of God, enjoy his creation, and live thoughtful, intentional lives. These great priorities will not happen by accident—we must clear out the clutter and spend time alone with the Lord each day.

Prayer

God, thank you for your Word. It is a lamp to my feet and a light to my path. I want to grow in wisdom and maturity, Father, so please teach me from your Scriptures. As I sit to read the Bible, please prepare my heart to hear what you have to say. Help me have the courage of spirit to obey what I read. Amen.

1. J. S. Brooker, ed., *T. S. Eliot: The Contemporary Reviews* (Cambridge: Cambridge University Press, 2004), 310.

10

HEIGHTENED AWARENESS

Scripture Passage: *"The fear of the LORD is the beginning of knowledge; fools despise wisdom and instruction."* —Proverbs 1:7

READ: ECCLESIASTES 12:11–14

I've done a lot of foolish things in my life, and sneaking up on a nine-hundred-pound grizzly bear with only a bow and arrow might top the list. I can still remember the feeling of my heart pounding in my chest and the sound of my arrow rattling on its rest. As I looked into those beady eyes, I remembered that I was in central Alaska, approximately three hundred miles from the nearest hospital and a rapid blood infusion device. My guide was carrying a Remington 7mm mag, but I was thirty yards in front of him. We had crawled through wild blueberries and spongy tundra to within about 125 yards of the bear. That's as close as we could get—there wasn't another bush or stump between us. To advance farther would be to leave the category of "foolish" for the category of "suicidal," and I wasn't willing to make that leap.

Fear is a funny thing. It drives us toward certain things and away from others. The Scriptures tell us that in order to live well and fully, we must fear the Lord. Fearing the Lord is very different than fearing an animal that would take great pleasure in eating you. Fear of a bear makes you afraid of getting too close. Fear of the Lord makes you afraid of not getting close enough to him. To fear the Lord is to appreciate the power, wonder, and mystery of God in a way that causes us to long to be near him and to dread being separated from him.

Psalm 31:19 describes how, if we fear God, we long to run to him: "Oh, how abundant is your goodness, which you have stored up for those who fear you and worked for those who take refuge in you, in the sight of the children of mankind!"

There is also an important similarity between fearing a bear and fearing the Lord: both fears cause us to be intensely aware of who we are with and what we are doing. When I was near the grizzly, I was acutely aware of him. I measured every move, paying attention not only to the bear but also to my breathing, my actions, and my thoughts. When we fear the Lord, we live with similar urgency and intentionality. Because we are always in God's presence, every thought and action counts. He is an awesome being, infinitely perfect and holy in all his ways.

The most appropriate response to being in God's presence is fear and reverence. As Eugene Peterson suggests, "Fear-of-the-Lord keeps us on our toes in the play of creation, keeps our eyes open—something's going on here and I don't want to miss it."[1]

Both God and the bear are unpredictable, but God will never do anything harmful toward one of his children. He's infinitely powerful and utterly untamable. Yet, all his ways are good, and he only brings about what is best for those who love him. Our joy is in carrying a heightened awareness of our awesome God.

Prayer

Almighty God, I pray that you would place within my heart a reverence and respect for you that is greater than my reverence and respect for all other things. You are the one true God who is worthy of my fear, and I long to be with you. Amen.

1. Eugene Peterson, *Christ Plays in Ten Thousand Places: A Conversation in Spiritual Theology* (Grand Rapids: Eerdmans, 2005), 122.

11

THE SMELL OF FISH

Scripture Passage: *"For his eyes are on the ways of a man, and he sees all his steps."* —Job 34:21

READ: JONAH

Fish never smelled so sweet. The summer before my senior year of high school, my friend Thom and I went to Canada to fish for walleye and northern pike. Day after day, we woke up early, caught a mess of fish, and then ate those fish for dinner. We went to bed early most nights, without showering, in order to wake up and repeat this perfect routine the following day. After a week of catching, cleaning, and eating fish, everything about us smelled like those slippery creatures. Our stench was testimony to the fun we'd had every day that week.

Jonah also smelled like fish, but it didn't smell sweet to him. Jonah's fishiness reminded him of his failed attempt to escape God's vision. God sent Jonah on a mission: "Arise, go to Nineveh, that great city, and call out against it, for their evil has come up before me" (Jon. 1:2).

Jonah didn't like this command, so he ran—or rather, he sailed. He caught a ride on a ship bound for someplace far away from God's line of sight, or so he thought. Not until Jonah was vomited onto a beach after spending three days inside the belly of a large fish did he learn that he could never escape the vision of God.

One of the reasons that we men end up in sticky, painful situations is that we lose sight of this vital truth: God sees everything. There is no place where his vision isn't perfect, discerning the thoughts, actions, and words of all people. Some might think this is an awful truth, but it's not. In fact, it's utterly good and beneficial that God sees everything. Sin leads to death, so the fact that God sees our sins, corrects us, and helps us turn from them is a life-giving gift. When the Bible presents God's perfect vision, it is meant to be an encouragement. "For the eyes of the LORD run to and fro throughout the whole earth, to give strong support to those whose heart is blameless toward him" (2 Chron. 16:9).

I don't want to be like Jonah—he never reached a point where the perfect, loving eyes of God seemed like a good thing. Even though he eventually obeyed God, we learn that he ends up sitting on a hill, reeking of fish, and pouting about God's mercy and grace toward his enemies, the Ninevites. The Ninevites, however, are throwing a huge party and giving thanks to God for seeing them in their sin and sending Jonah to warn them. They came to experience a relationship with an all-seeing, loving, and gracious God. What does God's perfect vision mean to you?

Prayer

Father, give me a heart that delights in your perfect vision. Help me trust that all your thoughts and ways toward me are good. May this truth cause me to be humble, and not fearful of your role in my life. Help me sense that you are with me every moment of my life, correcting me when I make sinful choices. Amen.

12

FUNNY STUFF

Scripture Passage: *"Let no corrupting talk come out of your mouths, but only such as is good for building up, as fits the occasion, that it may give grace to those who hear."* —Ephesians 4:29

READ: EPHESIANS 5:1–5

My fishing buddy Mark is a riot. We'll spend three hours cruising around a lake, throwing spinners, worms, and stick baits for bass, and by the time we dock the boat, my cheeks and my sides ache with laughter. As much as I enjoy catching fish, my favorite part of fishing with Mark is laughing at his well-timed, perfectly crafted one-liners. Like a crackling fire on a snowy night, certain people can fill a room with warmth by the jokes they tell. People who have a good sense of humor are a source of delight to those around them. Mark Twain said, "Humor is mankind's greatest blessing."

However, this blessing can become a curse. I was at a dinner party awhile back and several couples were standing by the tables of food, talking and laughing. One husband's voice rose above the rest, gaining the floor and the attention of everyone around the table. He told a joke about his wife's ineptness in the kitchen, which solicited laughs from the other people in the room. His wife took a step back from the table, sheepishly looked around the room, and tried to feign a smile. The man went on to tell a few more jokes about his wife's struggles in the home. His wife continued to back up, eventually exiting the dining room and retreating to the kitchen to do the dishes.

A sense of humor is a powerful tool. And like all tools, it can be used for good or for harm. Humor is positive when we use it to lift someone's spirits or laugh at the things in life worth laughing at. But humor is harmful when we use it to deflect a serious conversation or to laugh at things in life that are not meant to be funny. As the wife at the dinner party can attest, sarcasm can create or reopen deep wounds.

Let me suggest that we view our humor in the same way we view the last arrow in our quiver or the lone shotgun shell in our pocket. I was on a mule deer hunt a few years ago that drained my quiver. By midmorning, I found myself in the middle of Unit 2B in northern New Mexico, surrounded by large mulies, with one arrow left in my quiver. I was intensely aware that I needed to make that arrow count. We should view our humor in this same manner, realizing its power and how, when used appropriately, it can lead to great things. Yet, we should be cautious about pulling it out and using it thoughtlessly. Every word should count because once fired, we can't get it back—it's out there, for good or for harm.

Be funny, my friends. But aim true.

Prayer

Holy Spirit, help me to see when my sense of humor encourages and builds others up and when it tears others down. Please convict me of any sarcasm or inappropriate expressions of humor that might downgrade other people. Give me the ability to make people laugh in positive, productive ways that glorify you. Amen.

13

STICKY HANDS, CLEAN HEARTS

Scripture Passage: *"Create in me a clean heart, O God, and renew a right spirit within me."* —Psalm 51:10

READ: MARK 7:1–23

Our family often holds hands when we pray for a meal. My son sits to my left, and holding his hand is like gripping warm flypaper. It's sticky and smells like toad, ball glove, or dog hair. I'm pretty sure it has flies stuck to it occasionally.

You should also know that I'm a bit of a germophobe. When I studied biology in college, I developed a mild case of misophobia, a fear of germs and dirt. I buy antibacterial soap in bulk, hit the hand sanitizer obsessively, and tell our kids to "Wash your hands!" nonstop. The other night when my son glued his hand to mine at the dinner table, I started lecturing him on the importance of washing his hands before he eats. He could have washed his hands ten times in the time it took me to reeducate him on the necessity of proper hygiene.

Later that night I read the kids a Bible story from Mark 7:1–23, and I felt a wee bit challenged. Jesus and his disciples were eating dinner without washing their hands, and the religious leaders made a tremendous fuss over it. Jesus responded to them: "There is nothing outside a person that by going into him can defile him, but the things that come out of a person are what defile him" (Mark 7:15).

What an amazing statement about the kingdom of God. Religious people and hypocrites focus on rules and rituals, thinking that people are either "clean" or "dirty" by their performance in religious rites. However, people who walk in relationship with God know that they are either "clean" or "dirty" depending on the status of their hearts. If their hearts are full of faith and love toward God, then they are clean and healthy. If their hearts are hard toward God and they are looking to the work of their hands to make them worthy, they are dirty through and through.

A person who walks by faith in the grace of God could spend all day rolling around in cow pies in western Nebraska and still be clean if his heart has been made pure by the gospel of grace. Likewise, you can eat the cleanest cracker on a sterilized plate, but if your heart is sick with sin and self, you are defiled before God. This truth doesn't let us off the hook from washing our hands before dinner, but it does remind us that we must keep our focus on the heart.

If the heart has been made clean by grace through faith in Jesus, the entire person is clean. Even if his hands smell like toads, ball gloves, and dog hair.

Prayer

Father, help me focus on my heart and not my outer appearance. I want to be clean and whole inside, by your grace and mercy. Father, help me to be the type of husband, father, and friend who focuses on the heart as I relate with other people. Help me encourage others to worship you with their heart, soul, mind, and strength. Amen.

14

WADING INTO
THE WATERS

Scripture Passage: *"Oh, taste and see that the* LORD *is good! Blessed is the man who takes refuge in him!"* —Psalm 34:8

READ: JOHN 12:20-26

Fly rod sales skyrocketed in 1992 thanks to the movie *A River Runs Through It*. As people watched the film in air-conditioned theaters, they envisioned wading into raging rivers and artistically presenting dry flies, nymphs, and midges to unsuspecting trout. I worked in the fishing department of a sporting goods store when this movie hit theaters. The day after it released, we had a line an hour long. Even women and children wanted to learn how to set up a fly rod.

God designed our hearts so that images and pictures move us. If a vision connects with our soul, we are inspired to act. The opposite is also true; if we are vision*less*, we tend to do nothing. We especially need vision when it comes to how to live life with God. Proverbs 29:18 states, "Where there is no prophetic vision the people cast off restraint, but blessed is he who keeps the law."

Just as the movie *A River Runs Through It* presents powerful pictures of fly-fishing, the Bible presents powerful images of what it looks like to be in a relationship with Jesus. Christianity is an active faith-system; we weren't meant to sit back and watch others live it out. Much like watching others catch trout can't touch the joys of actually reeling one in for yourself, reading stories of faithful people can't compare to the exhilaration of your own walking by faith in the grace of God.

God wants to be known, experienced, and apprehended by us. He wants us to experience him. In fact, the Bible uses sensory language to show us that we can experience him. Psalm 34:8 states,

"Oh, taste and see that the LORD is good!" Jesus said, "Blessed are the pure in heart, for they shall see God" (Matt. 5:8). He also said, "Blessed rather are those who hear the word of God and keep it!" (Luke 11:28). *Taste, see, hear*—these are sensory allusions that show us that we can know God in real and tangible ways. They encourage us to engage God in every moment of our day.

As A. W. Tozer writes, "A spiritual kingdom lies all about us, enclosing us, embracing us, altogether within reach of our inner selves, waiting for us to recognize it. God Himself is here waiting our response to His presence. This eternal world will come alive to us the moment we begin to reckon upon its reality."[1]

Wade into the waters, brothers. Don't sit back and watch others know the joy of walking with Christ. Gear up. Grab your Bible, plug into a church, and learn the pleasure of knowing Christ. If you pursue God, he will show himself to you. And there's no adventure quite like pursuing God.

Prayer

Father, help me catch a vision for walking closely with you each day. Help me understand that I can know you in practical, real, everyday ways. Please make your presence known to me as I seek you in your Word. I look forward to our time together, Father. Amen.

1. A. W. Tozer, *The Pursuit of God* (Camp Hill, PA: Christian Publications, 1982), 52.

15

STOP YOUR WHINING

Scripture Passage: *"And the people complained in the hearing of the LORD about their misfortunes, and when the LORD heard it, his anger was kindled, and the fire of the LORD burned among them and consumed some outlying parts of the camp."* —Numbers 11:1

READ: PHILIPPIANS 2:14–15

A few years ago, I hunted longbeards along the Oregon coastline. I was with a group of professionals from the outdoor industry. The companies that hosted the event spared no expense placing us in comfy accommodations, partnering us with skilled guides, and putting us into some of the most breathtaking environments Oregon has to offer.

One night, after feasting on wild game, I sat by a roaring fire and chatted with six other hunters. Disregarding the rules about polite company, we talked about politics, the outdoor industry, and religion. A few of the men complained the entire night; according to them, the president was a failure, the outdoor industry was falling apart, and all churches were filled with hypocrites. As we moved from one topic to another, a fog of cynicism mixed with the wood smoke and made the air feel thick.

One of the men, Joel, participated in the conversations but never complained. He asked good questions, listened well, and at times challenged the other men in what they were saying. But his challenges were playful and nonthreatening. Joel's presence helped fight back the fog and steer the conversation in productive directions.

At the end of the evening, I asked Joel why he refused to join the other men in their complaining. He replied, "If I grumble and complain, how will the world know that I'm a Christian?" Joel's response reminded me of Philippians 2:14–15: "Do all things without grumbling or disputing, that you may be blameless and innocent, children of God."

It feels so natural and easy to complain and grumble. We all know that there is something broken and flawed about every person, place, and situation, so why not complain about it? However, there is a high cost to complaining when we are Christians: when we whine, we communicate to the world that we do not enjoy the goodness of God. We have the presence of God with us at all times. And as Psalm 16:11 reminds us, where God is, there is pleasure: "In [His] presence there is fullness of joy; at [His] right hand are pleasures forevermore." How will others know about the joy of the Lord if we are known by our grumbling? Equally important, how will we enjoy the Lord if all we do is focus on what we think is wrong?

At the end of the turkey hunting trip, as we were loading bags into the trailer, one of the hunters pulled Joel aside and thanked him for being in camp. He said, "I can't explain it, Joel . . . but having you in camp was a breath of fresh air."

Prayer

Jesus, help me to have a heart that genuinely enjoys the life you have given me. When things aren't going well at work or in our country, help me still find pleasures at your right hand forever. Father, help me to honor you by the way I use my mouth—not to complain but to give thanks, acknowledging and appreciating your good gifts. Amen.

16

NEW EVERY DAY

Scripture Passage: *"The steadfast love of the LORD
never ceases; his mercies never come to an end; they
are new every morning; great is your faithfulness."*
—Lamentations 3:22–23

READ: MATTHEW 6:25–34

Alaska has countless ways to steal a man's life, and my friend Rich-
ard encountered one of them. He was hunting moose by himself
on the second day of a ten-day trip. As he walked along the rim
of a canyon, the rocks beneath his feet gave way. He fell 150 feet
before a rocky outcrop jutting from the side of the mountain caught
him. He broke both his legs and cracked his pelvis. He was alone,
and nobody would miss him for eight more days.

Rich's daypack was still on his back. He had sixty-four ounces
of water, two granola bars, and a small bottle of ibuprofen. In the
hours following the accident, Rich's shock produced an intense
hunger and thirst. He ate both granola bars. He rationed the water,
planning to drink no more than fifteen ounces per day. And then
he waited, sitting motionless on that ledge in the middle of Alaska.
Three days after the fall, a commercial jet flew overhead and Rich
made contact with the pilot using his two-way radio. The pilot
radioed Anchorage, and an emergency helicopter rescued Rich
six hours later.

After the accident, Rich described those three days of waiting
as the most intensely vulnerable four thousand minutes of his life.
All he could do, every moment, was wait for God to give him what
he needed next. For three days, God kept Rich alive.

There is a statement in Lamentations that speaks to those who
are vulnerable and in need. Lamentations 3:22–23 says, "The steadfast love of the LORD never ceases; his mercies never come to an

end; they are new every morning; great is your faithfulness." As I counsel people who are going through relational, spiritual, or physical trauma, one of the most common statements I hear is, "I'm overwhelmed! I can't make it through this."

Despair is often the result of trying to comprehend the needs of tomorrow and how we, in our strength, will meet those needs. But Lamentations reminds us that our survival and joy don't work that way. They come about through faith and the belief that God will give us what we need for today.

When we have those overwhelming feelings of worry about where tomorrow's help will come from, we remind ourselves that the help will come from the Lord—tomorrow, when we need it, and no sooner. We know from the Scriptures and from our past experiences that God gives us just enough mercy and strength to make it through the moment. What he asks from us is to trust that his love and mercies will never end. He doesn't give us today what is needed for tomorrow. Those mercies show up in the morning. He promises.

Prayer

God, thank you that your mercies are new every single day. Help me see your grace and help today and not feel anxious about tomorrow. Produce in me a deep trust that you will show up afresh in each rising of the sun, and that you will be faithful to me tomorrow just as you were today. Amen.

17

BLOODSHED

Scripture Passage: *"For if the blood of goats and bulls, and the sprinkling of defiled persons with the ashes of a heifer, sanctify for the purification of the flesh, how much more will the blood of Christ, who through the eternal Spirit offered himself without blemish to God, purify our conscience from dead works to serve the living God."* —Hebrews 9:13–14

READ: EXODUS 12:1-13

I'll never forget the first time I field-dressed a deer. It was a small, basket-racked buck from the Nebraska Sandhills. I was by myself, and I had never hunted, shot, or cleaned an animal that large before. As I knelt beside the deer's body, I slowly made an incision from the groin to the sternum. The bullet had penetrated both lungs and had emptied bright red blood into the chest cavity. When I finished my cut and rolled the deer onto its side, blood rushed out of the body and over my boots. I could feel the warmth through the rubber covering the top of my foot. I sat down on the hill and spent several moments contemplating the loss of life represented in the growing pool of blood on that green hill in Garfield County. The moment was surreal, and I felt somber.

I wonder if this is how the Israelite families felt when they had to slaughter sheep on that dreadful Passover night? God was gracious in sending Egypt the first nine plagues. These plagues showed that Israel's God was the one true God and that Egypt's gods were powerless. The plague of blood in the river proved that Egypt's river god was a fake. The plague of the locusts showed that their god of the harvest was impotent. The Egyptians developed boils that wouldn't heal, demonstrating that their god of healing was unable to help them. The first nine plagues offered Egypt a chance to turn to the Lord, but Pharaoh didn't heed the warning. And so the final, terrible plague was issued: the death of every firstborn son.

The angel of death visited the entire land of Egypt, including the Israelite homes. When God decided to judge sin in Egypt, both the Egyptians and Israelites had reason to fear. Both groups had been worshiping idols. Yet, in an act of mercy toward Israel, God provided a way of escape—a way that involved a lot of blood. Each home would choose a lamb from their flock. They would keep the lamb inside with the family for four days, feeding it, caring for it, and protecting it as if their own lives depended on its survival . . . because they did. Then, on the day of judgment, the patriarch of the family would take the spotless lamb into his arms, gently hold back its head, and slit its throat with a knife. The lamb's blood was collected and painted on the doorposts of the house.

That night, as the family huddled together in their home, the angel of death visited the land. The angel would take the life of the firstborn son from every house in Egypt. But if the angel visited a house that had the blood of the lamb on its doorposts, he would pass over that house. The lamb's blood would be credited to the firstborn as a substitute.

Several thousand years later, Jesus, the perfect Lamb of God, shed his blood for our sins. Jesus's blood, being infinitely more precious and valuable than the blood of a lamb, atoned for our sins once and for all. In that gruesome moment, as the blood of God spilled onto a Roman cross, Jesus became our substitute. If you trust in Jesus as Lord, his blood satisfies the wrath of God and, as with the firstborn sons of Israel, spares the lives that should have been taken—yours and mine.

Prayer

Merciful heavenly Father, thank you for sending your Son to die on a cross to be a payment for my sins. I trust that Jesus is God, and as such, his blood is infinitely valuable and able to atone for my sins once and for all. I place my faith in Jesus, and I thank you for your immeasurable grace and mercy toward me. Amen.

18

A GOOD SUBMISSION

Scripture Passage: *"Agree with God, and be at peace; thereby good will come to you."* —Job 22:21

READ: 1 PETER 2:13–3:7

When most men hear the word "submit," they think of what a hunting dog does when its master sends a couple volts into its collar, or when an MMA fighter is placed in an arm bar or a rear naked choke. Submission isn't a popular idea today because it signifies being forced to do something by someone more powerful than you, often painfully. But the biblical picture of submission is different; it's a decision motivated by faith and trust in God, producing peace and contentment for those who practice it.

The *natural man* who lives his life apart from God views and practices submission differently than the man who walks by faith. For the natural man, an outside force, such as a person or an organization, drives and demands his submission. He is often made to submit by the threat of consequences or the promise of rewards.

Conversely, the *spiritual man* who walks with God views submission as internally driven and heart motivated. For him it is a means to relate well with God and others.

The natural man views the structures of authority as a representation of worth and value. He believes that those who are in charge are worth more than those who are subordinate, whereas the spiritual man knows that every person is made in the image of God and is equally valuable. For the spiritual man, the choice to submit is not the choice to surrender self-worth.

Perhaps the core difference in these conflicting perspectives of submission is that the man apart from the Spirit believes life revolves around *him*. His priority is to control people and situations as much as possible in order to find pleasure and significance.

Submission is therefore a hindrance in his attempt to "master his own destiny." But the Spirit-filled man believes that life is oriented around *God*. He enjoys freedom from worrying about control and influence, and this freedom enables him to trust in the character of God no matter what people and institutions are in authority over him.

I recently hunted geese with a wise old sportsman who is nearing the last season of his life. As we sat in the blind, drinking cheap coffee and watching mice scurry back and forth over the tops of our boots, we talked about how different heaven will be from life on earth right now. He said, "I've always believed that, if it's going to happen in heaven, let it happen now." This attitude applies well to the idea of submission. Heaven will not contain struggle, envy, or greed. It will not contain ego-driven competition. Yet, it will contain submission. Philippians 2:10 reminds us of this truth: "So that at the name of Jesus every knee should bow, in heaven and on earth and under the earth." If submission is an essential part of the pleasure we will have in eternity, then it certainly plays a key role in enjoying life right now.

Prayer

Father, out of reverence and respect for you, help me submit to the authority you have placed in my life. Help me to do this with a glad heart and a willing spirit, not with bitterness and resentment. Please help me to speak with respect and graciousness about the people and institutions you have established. Amen.

19

No Nipping Zone

Scripture Passage: *"Death and life are in the power of the tongue, and those who love it will eat its fruits."* —Proverbs 18:21

READ: GENESIS 2:18–25

Nobody likes to be nipped at all the time. Just ask our family dog, Ezra. We got an eight-week-old yellow Labrador puppy a few weeks ago, and she will not stop biting, jumping on, and tormenting ol' Ez. These two pups have several years of sharing a dog run ahead of them, and nipping isn't helping Hazel kick things off on the right paw.

Nipping isn't a great strategy for marriage, either. Couples who constantly criticize and nag one another have toxic, energy-depleting marriages. I counseled a husband and wife recently. The husband spent thirty minutes criticizing his wife on everything from keeping a dirty house, to not letting him spend money on hunting gear, to never letting him spend time with his friends. The wife spent her half of the session attacking him for leaving his clothes around the house, never taking her on dates, and spending hours in the woods when he could be spending time with the kids. By the end of the session, these two were covered in welts and teeth marks from all the nipping, biting, and chewing.

We have a proverb in our culture today that simply isn't true: *Sticks and stones may break my bones, but words will never hurt me.* It has a good ring to it, but it's far from the truth. Words, according to the Bible, hold the power of life and death. What we say to our spouse either imparts life or steals it. When a husband says to his wife, "You are beautiful inside and out, and I'm so thankful to have you in my life," he shapes his wife's view of herself. A wife who knows she is loved has a greater capacity to love her husband. This means that a husband who speaks kindly to his wife does himself a big favor: "He who loves his wife loves himself" (Eph. 5:28).

The stakes are high when it comes to nipping. A week after we put Hazel in the kennel with Ezra, Ezra took off into a cornfield and didn't look back. His goal: shake the little yellow pest that had kept him from peace. We eventually found our frustrated dog a couple fields from home and returned him to the kennel. He and Hazel overcame what was a rough start to their relationship. I don't usually see the same turnaround in marriages when people spend years hurting each other with their words. Usually one person, or sometimes both, gets tired of the biting, and they run.

But it doesn't have to be this way. Good marriages and healthy homes are possible. Success often comes down to whether or not we, as husbands and fathers, choose to speak in a way that builds up and encourages others. Our words will contain the power of life if we choose them wisely.

Prayer

Father, keep me from nipping at the people I love. Help me to use my words to build up and give grace to those who hear me speak. Help me to have a marriage that is characterized by peace and love, and help me to lead my wife and family in this direction. Amen.

20

TRANSFORMATION

Scripture Passage: *"And we all, with unveiled face, beholding the glory of the Lord, are being transformed into the same image from one degree of glory to another. For this comes from the Lord who is the Spirit."*
—2 Corinthians 3:18

READ: ROMANS 6:19–23

Men have used camouflage clothing to blend in with their surroundings since World War I. Abbot Thayer's book *Concealing Coloration in the Animal Kingdom* (published in 1909) helped the American military develop the idea of using clothing to mimic the terrain and protect our troops from bombs and bullets. Bright, splendid military attire made men on the battlefields vulnerable to attack. Camouflage was the solution.

In the late 1970s, sportsman Jim Crumley caught onto the idea of using our clothing to blend into nature. He tie-dyed some pants and jackets, then used magic markers to draw vertical lines.[1] The final product looked like the trunk of a tree, so Crumley named it "Trebark." This new camouflage revolutionized hunting, and sportsmen have been wearing camouflage ever since.

Camouflage helps a man with external change, but the Spirit of God takes a man through a complete metamorphosis, as Paul says in 2 Corinthians 3:18. At the moment we place our faith in Christ, the Holy Spirit enters our soul and begins the slow and steady work of changing our inner lives to become more like Jesus. He frees us from sinful habits and traits. He renews our thoughts and feelings. He develops within us a passion for the things of God and the character of Christ. In the same way putting on a

IN PURSUIT

1. M. J. Stephey, *A Brief History of Camouflage*, http://www.time.com/time/nation/article/0,8599,1906083,00.html.

camouflage sweatshirt makes us look like our natural surroundings, putting on the Lord Jesus Christ by faith (see Rom. 13:14) causes us to think, feel, act, and speak like Jesus.

We have a vital role to play in this act of transformation. We must agree with this work and cooperate with the Holy Spirit. In his book *The Discipline of Grace*, Jerry Bridges writes, "Though sanctification is the work of the Holy Spirit in us, it does involve our wholehearted response in obedience and the regular use of the spiritual disciplines that are instruments of sanctification."[2] God makes us more like Christ, but we join him in the work through our obedience and faithfulness.

Sanctification is a long process. A man can slip on a set of camouflage clothing in ten minutes and look like a tree or a bush. But the man who desires to be like Christ will be experiencing ongoing transformation throughout his entire life. We all have a long way to go in thinking, feeling, and acting like Jesus. That's fine—we have a God who not only changes lives but who also shows incredible patience as he takes us through the process.

Prayer

Holy Spirit, continue your work of making me into the image of Jesus. I invite you to change my heart, my thoughts, my feelings, my actions, and my relationships. If there is anything about me that doesn't look like Christ, I invite you to do your work of change. Amen.

2. Jerry Bridges, *The Discipline of Grace: God's Role and Our Role in the Pursuit of Holiness* (Colorado Springs: NavPress, 2006), 96.

21

"That's My Dad"

Scripture Passage: *"But to all who did receive him, who believed in his name, he gave the right to become children of God."* —John 1:12

Read: Romans 8:13–17

The other morning I went to pick up my son from a birthday party at a friend's house. As I pulled up to the farm, I saw Aidan shooting .22 rifles with several boys and fathers. As I walked toward the field, one of Aidan's friends called out, "Hi, Pastor Zeke!"

That got my son's attention. He spun around, set the gun down, and ran over to me. "Dad, watch this!"

He walked back to the line, picked up the rifle, and shot the metal target in the center. A few moments later, as we climbed into the truck, Aidan put his hand on my forearm and squeezed. "Did you see that shot, Dad? I did that *for you*."

We can accomplish amazing things when we know our father is watching us with a sense of pride and acceptance. Moments like that one with my son remind me of the power and presence of a father. They also remind me that there was a time when I didn't know God as my Father.

In the spiritual realm, we all started off fatherless, like homeless children living on the streets. Ephesians 2:3 reminds us that we "were by nature children of wrath, like the rest of mankind." There was nothing endearing about us; we weren't cute, cuddly, or exceptional in our skills and abilities. God didn't turn his eye toward us because we did something right. He chose to adopt us into his family so that we would experience and appreciate the riches of his mercy and grace. Twice in Ephesians 1:12–14, Paul tells us that God chose us so that we would "be to the praise of [God's] glory." What an amazing thought—God saved us so that our joy would echo into the expanses of the universe, and so all would see the works of the Lord and praise him.

If you've placed your faith in Jesus, you are now a son or daughter of God. When you pray, you should view it as a family conversation. You would never look at the floor and talk sheepishly to your father on earth as if you didn't know him; neither should you act like you don't belong in the family of God. Like my son who couldn't wait to run to me and get my attention, we can approach God with boldness, heading into each day with a sense that he is watching us with pride and acceptance. As the hymn "All the Way My Savior Leads Me" celebrates, "He cheers each winding path [you] tread."

Prayer

Father, I didn't deserve to be your child, but I cannot imagine life without you as my Dad. Thank you for the grace and mercy you have shown me. Help me see you as my Father and approach you without any reservation or shame. Amen.

22

THE WINNING SIDE

Scripture Passage: *"'Because the poor are plundered, because the needy groan, I will now arise,' says the LORD; 'I will place him in the safety for which he longs.'"*
—Psalm 12:5

READ: MICAH 6:6–8

Several years ago, I participated in a quail shoot in which twelve teams of two shooters each worked their way through a quarter section of switchgrass, taking as many quail as possible. When I first arrived at the event, I spotted a man in the parking lot who I knew was an excellent shot. I'd hunted with Jeff before, and when he carried his short-barreled American Arms over-under, birds were going to drop. I approached Jeff, asked him to be my partner, and two hours later we divvied up the prize money. We all want to be aligned with the strong and victorious.

Nobody is stronger than God. And when it comes to God's determination to care for suffering people, nobody will stand in his way. He will be victorious in providing for those in need. Timothy Keller stated this truth in a sermon:

> One of the great themes of the Hebrew Scriptures is that God identifies with the suffering. There are all these great texts that say things like this: If you oppress the poor, you oppress me. I am a husband to the widow. I am father to the fatherless. I think the texts are saying God binds up his heart so closely with suffering people that he interprets any move against them as a move against him.[1]

1. Steve McCoy, "Tim Keller & 9/11 Remembrance Message," *Reformissionary* (blog), September 19, 2008, http://www.stevekmccoy.com/reformissionary/2006/09/tim_keller_911_.html.

IN PURSUIT

62

"God binds up his heart so closely with suffering people" is a great description of Psalm 35:10: "O Lord, who is like you, delivering the poor from him who is too strong for him, the poor and needy from him who robs him?" God will not step aside and do nothing while vulnerable people are hurt and abused. He will fight for them, and he will win. Many Christians believe this, and yet they fail to ask the vital "how" question.

How does he plan to save the sex slave in Sri Lanka?

How will he provide care for the child with AIDS in Nigeria?

How will he feed and provide shelter to the foster children in America?

When a man asks the "how" question, he finds an answer that will change his life. Isaiah 1:17 reveals God's strategy: "Learn to do good; seek justice, correct oppression; bring justice to the fatherless, plead the widow's cause." He wants you and me to race to the side of the needy.

We must not let the enormity and complexity of the world's problems keep us from a simple, yet vital act of faith and help. If a sportsman and his family will identify a person in need and then get involved through prayer, giving money, or adoption, lives will be changed. Do you want to be on the winning team, on the side of strength, dedication, and victory? Our God will rescue, and he will judge and punish wickedness. There's nothing more dynamic and powerful than God's plan to rescue hurting people. And he's inviting you to be on his team.

*P*rayer

God, give me a heart that feels what you feel for those in need. Help me not give up or get discouraged by the scope of the problem. Give me the simple faith to find a person in need who I can help. I want to be on your team, helping you rescue hurting people. Amen.

23

CROWNS OF GRAY

Scripture Passage: *"The glory of young men is their strength, but the splendor of old men is their gray hair."* —Proverbs 20:29

READ: JOB 12:12-25

I recently helped lead a youth bowhunter camp. For five days, young men and women between eight and sixteen years of age launched arrows at foam targets, practiced with game calls, and learned how to hunt from tree stands and ground blinds. Throughout the week, the big issue was draw weight, or the poundage they could handle as they pulled back their bows. Each kid wanted to see how strong they were and how their strength compared to the other shooters. On the first day, a fifteen-year-old boy stepped up to the rack of bows, grabbed the heaviest, and pulled it back with ease. His triceps rippled as he launched the arrow. This young man was treated as a god all week.

Solomon, the wise king of ancient Israel, wrote, "The glory of young men is in their strength, but the splendor of old men is their gray hair" (Prov. 20:29). Young men display their prowess through feats of strength—how much weight they can bench-press, how many logs they can carry in one trip to the woodshed, and how many pounds they can pull back when shooting a bow. In our world of youth and vigor, few things are honored more than physical prowess.

But eventually, the focus of a man's life must shift from strength to wisdom. Solomon uses "crowns of gray" imagery to symbolize wisdom and experience. Youth and strength are important, but the wisdom of the aged is more valuable because it is more costly to attain. Solomon explains how young men reach the wisdom and gray hair of the aged: "Blows that wound cleanse away evil; strokes make clean the innermost parts" (Prov. 20:30).

A crown of gray is achieved in large part through struggle and pain. The school of hard knocks enrolls reluctant students but produces mature graduates. The key to growing in wisdom involves more than simply going through difficulties—we must maintain a commitment to learning, growing, and changing throughout life.

When the young bowhunters left the archery range each afternoon, the older volunteers took their turn slinging arrows. I sat on a stool behind the line and watched as six graying men shot their trusty, familiar bows. As these friends slipped arrow after arrow into the center ring, I thought about their lives. Three men had buried a child. One recently went through a major heart operation. Another had endured a painful church split. All of them knew the bitter taste of suffering and hardship. But each of these men maintained a love for God, and the pain that threatened to do them in made them stronger and wiser. And left them with the gray hair to prove it.

Prayer

Father, thank you for the grace and strength to enjoy life. Thank you for my body and the opportunity it provides me to hunt and fish. May you deepen my desire for wisdom and give me the heart to learn the lessons you will teach me through the difficulties in life. Amen.

24

NOT FAIR

Scripture Passage: *"Why not rather suffer wrong? Why not rather be defrauded? But you yourselves wrong and defraud—even your own brothers!"* —1 Corinthians 6:7–8

READ: PHILIPPIANS 1:27–30

There's an innate longing in the human heart that makes us desire fairness and encourages us to cry "Foul!" when things don't go our way. This sense of fairness doesn't necessarily diminish as we grow older. I was at a deer check-in station a few years ago when a thirteen-year-old boy brought in a record-book buck. About six other hunters stood by the back of the pickup as the wide-eyed boy told his story. When the young hunter and his father drove away, one of the older men kicked a rock in the parking lot, shook his head, and stated, "It's not fair, I tell ya." Five other heads nodded in agreement.

It's not wrong to care about fairness. Justice is one of the essential attributes of God, and we exhibit Jesus's heart when we work for the fair treatment of other people. The problem isn't when we care that others are treated fairly. The problem occurs when we make fair treatment *for ourselves* our highest priority. It's impossible to love well when we are demanding our own rights.

Nobody knew unfair treatment better than the apostle Paul. When he wrote his letter to the church in Philippi, Paul was under house arrest in Rome. It was a false imprisonment based on bogus charges. Five years earlier, Paul had been worshiping God in the temple in Jerusalem. He was preaching to Jews and Gentiles that Jesus was the Messiah, which infuriated a group of Jewish men. They formed a mob, rushed into the temple, and dragged Paul out. The mob was stoning Paul when a Roman official stepped in and stopped the execution. He sent Paul to Caesarea, where Paul was imprisoned for two years. From there, Paul was sent to Rome, where he was imprisoned for two more years. For five years, someone else controlled Paul's life.

If anyone had the right to scream, "It's not fair!" it was Paul. Instead, he wrote a letter to the church in Philippi and said, "I want you to know, brothers, that what has happened to me has really served to advance the gospel, so that it has become known throughout the whole imperial guard and to all the rest that my imprisonment is for Christ" (Phil. 1:12–13).

Paul's our exemplar. After enduring five years of injustice at the hands of his persecutors, he said, "Don't worry about me. The gospel of Jesus Christ has moved forward!" And it had advanced—by the time Paul was finally released in AD 62, the best and brightest of Rome had become intimately familiar with the gospel of Jesus Christ. Paul had talked with dozens of the emperor's top officials and guards during his imprisonment. To Paul, that made all his suffering and unfair treatment worth it.

Are you being treated unfairly? Are you suffering unjustly because of your faith? If so, you're in good company. Paul would tell you to count it all joy because God is doing great things.

Prayer

My Lord, help me to know that you are in perfect control of my circumstances. When my heart wants to cry out, "It's not fair!" help me have the faith to say, "To God be the glory." Father, when others see my joy and peace in the middle of suffering, may they attribute the power to you. Amen.

25

PROTECT THIS HOUSE

Scripture Passage: *"Finally, brothers, whatever is true, whatever is honorable, whatever is just, whatever is pure, whatever is lovely, whatever is commendable, if there is any excellence, if there is anything worthy of praise, think about these things."* —Philippians 4:8

READ: 2 CORINTHIANS 10:1–6

We protect the places that matter most to us. We put armed guards in banks to protect our money. We keep satellites and aircraft in the sky to protect our country from terrorist attacks. We design our schools, churches, and homes in ways that make it difficult for others to harm our children. If we deem a certain place as important, we go to great lengths to protect what happens there. Yet, there is one vitally important place in our lives that often goes without careful guarding: our thoughts and feelings.

The Bible makes it clear that we are responsible for the ideas and images that we entertain in our heads. We can't completely control the thoughts that pop into our minds, but we can recognize whether they are healthy and then choose whether to dwell on them or not. The mind is treacherous terrain because there is genuine danger in entertaining thoughts that could hurt us.

For example, if we allow ourselves to view and dwell on violent, sexual, or deviant images, our hearts learn to tolerate, and eventually celebrate, sin. Over time, a steady stream of hurtful images can even lead us into a death of conscience. I once visited a college student in the hospital who had tried to commit suicide. He told me, "I've watched so many sick and twisted movies that my soul just feels dead inside. I just wanted to escape the images." The images we feed our minds hold the power to consume us. We must take this threat seriously.

In addition to thinking too much about violence, it's also dangerous to spend much time on ideas that put "me" at the center of the universe. I was in an archery store once when a customer, Bill, walked through the door, sat on the stool by the counter, and proceeded to tell everyone about his prowess as a bowhunter. He pulled out his phone and proved his point with pictures. It was a one-man show for forty-five minutes, and nobody else got a chance to talk. When Bill left, the owner of the store said to the other customers, "I'm sorry you had to go through that—Bill comes here every day to share the same stories and pictures with my customers."

Another area we must guard against is our feelings. We all feel things, and these emotions are important. But when we give our feelings decision-making power, we make choices we often regret. As followers of Christ, we need to examine our desires and emotions but not give them the ultimate position of authority in our lives. Author Oscar Wilde describes the attitude we ought to carry when he writes, "I don't want to be at the mercy of my emotions. I want to use them, to enjoy them, and to dominate them."[1]

The thought life is an important area of our lives that deserves our diligent care and concern. The Under Armour clothing company popularized the slogan "Protect This House." That phrase perfectly describes the attitude that we, as men seeking to follow Christ, must carry toward protecting our thought lives. Our minds are the first place we battle evil. We must aggressively and zealously choose to think upon the things of God. If we do, we will experience the promise of Isaiah 26:3: "You keep him in perfect peace whose mind is stayed on you, because he trusts in you."

Prayer

Father, help me to take my thought life seriously. Make me aware of which thoughts are good and helpful, and which thoughts threaten to steal my life and hurt my relationship with you. Give me the wisdom to know the truth and recognize what is false. For your glory and my good, I ask. Amen.

1. Oscar Wilde, *The Picture of Dorian Gray* (Plain Label Books), 228.

26

The Substitute Ram

Scripture Passage: *"For what does the Scripture say?*
'Abraham believed God, and it was counted to him as
righteousness.'" —Romans 4:3

READ: GENESIS 22:1–18

Just spotting a ram in the wild makes a sportsman giddy. Nebraska has a growing population of bighorn sheep. Hunters from around the Midwest drive to the northwest corner of my state on the off chance that they might even catch a glimpse of one of these majestic animals. That being said, no person in history was more excited to see a ram on a mountain than Israel's patriarch, Abraham. But Abraham's excitement had nothing to do with hunting. For him, the ram on the mountain meant that he would not have to carry out a very difficult command from God.

God tested Abraham's faith by telling him to go to the land of Moriah and sacrifice Isaac, his only son, on a mountain. This was a test like no other. God knew how much this father loved his boy. God even referred to Isaac as Abraham's "only son Isaac, whom you love" (Gen. 22:2). God knew the emotional difficulty in what he asked of Abraham. He also knew how intellectually and theologically challenging this test would be. Isaac was the child through whom God was going to make Abraham and his wife, Sarah, into the parents of many nations. Abraham had to be asking, "How can God require my son's life and still fulfill his promise?" The stage was set, and it was time to take the test: Would Abraham trust God to carry out his promise, even if it meant killing the very son through whom the promise was given?

We are given surprisingly few emotional details in this story. What we do see is that Abraham woke up early, saddled his donkey, gathered the wood for the journey, and traveled for three days to Moriah. *Three days!* For almost seventy-two hours, Abraham wrestled with this command before choosing to do what God commanded. Once they reached the mountain, Abraham took his son, placed him on the altar, and unsheathed his knife. His face was set on obeying God. God saw his faith and stopped the slaughter.

But God had required a sacrifice. Blood needed to be shed. So God provided a gift, a substitute: "And Abraham lifted up his eyes and looked, and behold, behind him was a ram, caught in a thicket by his horns. And Abraham went and took the ram and offered it up as a burnt offering instead of his son" (Gen. 22:13). Abraham and Isaac must have felt a mixture of relief and thanksgiving as they watched the blood flow from the ram onto the rocks of the mountain.

This story points us to Jesus and his Father. About two thousand years later, another Father walked his Son up a mountain to die as a sacrifice for sin. The mountain was Golgotha, and his Son was not spared the agony of slaughter. In a dramatic twist on the Isaac story, Jesus, the Son of God, was the substitute. The execution was intended for us: "For the wages of sin is death, but the free gift of God is eternal life in Christ Jesus our Lord" (Rom. 6:23). But Jesus, full of faith and promise, died in our place. Like Isaac, he carried the wood up the hill. Like Isaac, he was willing to allow his Father to take his life. And like Isaac, he obeyed because he trusted that his Father knew best. God does know best, and as sportsmen, all he requires of us is faith—the faith of Abraham, Isaac, and Jesus.

Prayer

Father, help me to trust in the sacrifice of Jesus for the forgiveness of my sins. I have a desire to trust in myself—my works, my abilities, my best efforts—but I know that Jesus's life and death alone can make things right between you and me. Help me to have the faith of Abraham, even when things don't make sense. Amen.

27

Rotten Bones

Scripture Passage: *"A tranquil heart gives life to the flesh, but envy makes the bones rot."* —Proverbs 14:30

Read: James 3:13–18

A man I know recently died of bone cancer. The disease slowly destroyed his bone marrow, leaving his arms brittle and weak. A couple months before his death, he shattered his wrist trying to open a jar of pickles. Cancer had eaten thousands of holes in his bones so that the X-rays looked like Swiss cheese.

Cancer isn't the only thing that rots our bones. According to Proverbs 14:30, few things are as sickening to our bodies as envy. If your buddy shoots a state-record buck and you wish you had made the shot instead, that's envy. Envy shows up in the Bible in several places. In Genesis, Cain murdered his brother, Abel, because he envied the favor God showed Abel and his offering. Jacob envied Esau's birthright, so he lied and deceived him. Even the crowd that pressured Pilate to kill Jesus acted out of envy: "For [Pilate] knew that it was out of envy that they had delivered him up" (Matt. 27:18). Envy is seen in someone who reacts negatively to the successes of others.

Envy is a sin that does nothing but eat away at our joy. While many sins present a false sense of pleasure or rush of adrenalin, envy doesn't even pretend to provide happiness. Lusting causes a rush of blood to the brain. Hurting others in our anger carries a sense of righting an injustice. Gluttony involves the fleeting pleasure of overindulging on something good. Many sins appeal to us because they *seem* to produce a sense of excitement. Envy is different; it only makes us feel empty and rotten inside.

A few years ago, a hunter from our area, James, shot the largest buck to be taken with a bow that year in Nebraska. The 6x6 nontypical whitetail scored almost 180 inches and weighed just over 200 pounds. James's friend, Greg, had been hunting the same property. The two had set up stands and trail cameras together, and they wished each other well and hoped that one would have success. When James shot the deer, Greg was the first person he called. Greg congratulated James, but in the months that followed, Greg pulled away. He grew bitter and envious, telling everyone around that he should have been the one to shoot that buck. Envy made his heart sick. It also ended his closest friendship. James told me recently, "I can't tell you how much I wish that Greg had shot that buck. I'd give it all up if I could get the friendship back."

The first step in defeating envy and restoring life to our bodies is recognizing when we're feeling it. If we sense our hearts recoiling when something good happens to someone else, we need to realize what we're doing and take seriously the threat that envy poses to our spiritual lives. Left unchecked, envy can take a healthy heart and turn it into something brittle, dry, and lifeless. But if we recognize our envy and ask God to help us celebrate the good that has happened to someone else, God will answer that prayer. He is, after all, the Great Physician.

Prayer

Jesus, help me have a healthy heart that doesn't envy the good things that happen to others. Help me stay tuned in to my heart so that I recognize envy when it springs up. And then, Father, give me the humility to confess my envy and let you give me a heart that celebrates the good things that happen to the people in my life. Amen.

28

The God of Governments

Scripture Passage: *"Let every person be subject to the governing authorities. For there is no authority except from God, and those that exist have been instituted by God."* —Romans 13:1

Read: 1 Peter 2:13–17

In March 2013, I had the privilege of opening the House of Representatives in prayer. As I stood at the same podium where our presidents give the State of the Union address, my heart pounded in my chest. I felt gratitude for the men and women who have served our country in the Capitol building since it opened in 1793. For over two hundred years, congressmen and congresswomen have passed laws, entered and exited wars, and helped ensure our rights and freedoms. I felt thankful to be a part of the greatest democracy in the world. Yet I also felt discouraged. Many of our leaders today are leading us away from the ethics of the kingdom of God.

Living as a Christian citizen in our country is not a simple issue, but the truth of 1 Peter 2:13–17 helps clarify our goal. Peter tells us to submit to our government leaders, respecting their positions and obeying their laws, because God is working through them to "punish those who do evil and to praise those who do good" (1 Pet. 2:14). This is not an easy command for us today because of all the evil that takes place in our nation. Yet, we must remember that it was not easy in Peter's day either; throughout his letter, Peter acknowledges that his audience was being treated cruelly because of their faith in Jesus. His recipients lived under a godless, tyrannical government, but Peter still instructed them to speak and act with respect. And so must we.

Right now antigun legislation is a priority issue. As sportsmen, we feel strongly about our government honoring our constitutional rights, especially in a day when the Second Amendment is under such attack. We have every right as citizens and Christians to stand up for what we believe. But we must do this in a way that respects our president and government officials. We are sportsmen, but even more importantly, we are Christians—people who are to be known for practicing truth and love. I occasionally receive emails from my sportsmen friends that attack our president in venomous, nonproductive ways. We all lose when this happens; if we dehumanize "the other side" or hurl insults at those in leadership, we ruin our testimony for Christ. It is possible to win an issue but lose the fight of faith, hope, and love.

As men of strength and courage, let us pray and work against evil. But let us also display the faith that recognizes God is in control of even corrupt nations, governments, and elected officials. And as Peter reminds us, we should praise God for our authorities when they carry out his justice and protection. I saw an example of this recently when the state of California mobilized various governmental agencies to track down and detain a fugitive, Christopher Dorner. Dorner was an ex-policeman who had killed three people and issued a manifesto in which he pledged to kill several other policemen and their families. Dorner fled to the Big Bear Mountains in California, where officials from the California Fish and Game Department discovered him. Thanks to courageous government agents, Dorner was unable to harm others before taking his own life.

For all of our government's flaws and failings, our sovereign God uses it every day to carry out and accomplish his purposes for our country. It's our role to trust the sovereign power of God and respect the authority he's put in place. By doing this, Peter tells us that we will "put to silence the ignorance of foolish people" (1 Pet. 2:15).

Prayer

Jesus, help me not to have a rebellious spirit against the authorities you have put in place over my life. Help me to know what it looks like to stand against evil in a respectful, winsome, and godly manner. Please continue to accomplish your purposes for our country through those leaders you have put in place. Amen.

29

LINKING TOGETHER

Scripture Passage: *"A friend loves at all times, and a brother is born for adversity."* —Proverbs 17:17

READ: ECCLESIASTES 4:9–12

Argentina is famous for excellent dove hunting. It's also infamous for fire ants. These tiny red insects are, pound for pound, tougher than you and I will ever be. They can survive almost anything nature throws at them—fire, pesticides, and even other bugs pose them little threat. Perhaps their most spectacular feature is their ability to survive a flood. These ants, which by themselves would drown in a matter of seconds, link together and form a pancake-like raft. This living raft traps air and keeps them afloat in the treacherous waters. As long as they link legs and hold on tight, the ants can survive floodwaters for months.[1]

Men are like fire ants when it comes to friendship. Proverbs 17:17 tells us that God gave us Christian friendship to help us through the difficult seasons in life. This was even true of Jesus. During his time on earth, our Savior had three close friends—Peter, James, and John—to walk with him through the most challenging, faith-testing moments of his life. These men prayed, laughed, and cried with him during his three-year ministry.

We were created to walk life's journey with a few close companions. However, we often try to substitute professional caregivers for friendship. As philosopher Ronald Dworkin has pointed out, the United States has witnessed a hundredfold increase in the number of professional caregivers since 1950. Our society boasts 77,000 clinical psychologists, 192,000 clinical social workers, 105,000 mental health counselors, 50,000 marriage and family therapists,

1. Amina Khan, "Mystery of Floating Fire Ants Solved," *Los Angeles Times*, April 29, 2011, http://articles.latimes.com/2011/apr/29/science/la-sci-ants-raft-20110430.

17,000 nurse psychotherapists, 30,000 life coaches, as well as hundreds of thousands of nonclinical social workers and substance abuse counselors. "Most of these professionals spend their days helping people cope with everyday life problems," Dworkin writes, "not true mental health issues."[2]

Many men don't need professional counseling. They need a good friend or two to link arms with during the trying times of life. Many men struggle to reach this depth of friendship; they have "buddies" they like to fish and hunt with, but when it comes to expressing pain or sadness, they feel like they are alone or isolated. It doesn't need to be this way.

Start with the guys you spend time with outdoors. Sitting in a duck blind or in the cab of a pickup as you drive west for an elk hunt can be great opportunities to connect about the deeper things in life. My main accountability partners are men with whom I bass fish and deer hunt. The relationships started out as purely recreational, but they developed into strong friendships because we began having intentional conversations about the hard things we were going through in life. You can have this as well, if you will initiate important topics and share your own struggles. Ask your friends to pray for you as you go through difficulties, and offer to pray for them. Adding this depth to a friendship may mean staying afloat when the floods come. It will also mean helping others stay afloat.

God's plan for helping us through adversity is a perfect one, but we've got to take the right steps to put our life raft in place.

Prayer

Father, help me to be a good friend to others. Help me be the kind of person who asks good questions, listens well, and then earnestly prays for my brothers. Father, please provide a good friend or two to encourage me, as well. Thank you for the gift of my brothers who are willing to stand by my side. Amen.

2. Ronald W. Dworkin, "The Rise of the Caring Industry," Stanford University's Hoover Institution website, June 1, 2010, http://www.hoover.org/publications/policy-review/article/5339.

30

NOBODY LIKE HIM

Scripture Passage: *"He is the image of the invisible God, the firstborn of all creation."* —Colossians 1:15

READ: HEBREWS 3:1–6

We all have heroes. When I was a new Christian in college, a pastor invited me to go bass fishing with him. Curt had sandwiches and sodas ready, so when I arrived we put the boat in and fished the last few hours of daylight. That was over twenty years ago, and I don't remember anything about the fishing. What I do remember is that, in about three hours of listening to Curt, I was given a vision of a new kind of man—someone who worshiped God more than God's creation, kept his family a greater priority than his work or favorite hobbies, and focused on other people's success more than his own. In three hours of "boat time," I had found an exemplar for how to live as a Christian sportsman.

When it comes to great men and women in the Scriptures, Moses ranks high on the list. Deuteronomy 34:10 records, "And there has not arisen a prophet since in Israel like Moses, whom the LORD knew face to face." Moses was a clear example of biblical leadership, humility, and courage. But for all Moses's glory, Jesus is infinitely superior: "For Jesus has been counted worthy of more glory than Moses—as much more glory as the builder of a house has more honor than the house itself" (Heb. 3:3). Moses led Israel out of Egyptian captivity; Jesus led God's people out of slavery to sin and death. Moses delivered the law of God, which showed people their inability to measure up to God; Jesus gave us the ministry of righteousness, making us fully pleasing to God by faith. And Moses was designed, created, and made great by God; Jesus, as God, was not designed, created, or made by anyone. He simply is, was, and always will be. Moses was a beautiful house that God had built; Jesus was the builder. There is no comparison.

We will meet extraordinary men in our lives. I've known a handful of guys like Curt in my lifetime, and they are extremely valuable to me. However, we will never encounter someone more interesting, powerful, and valuable than Jesus of Nazareth. He is wiser than Solomon, stronger than Samson, and more courageous than David. He is the image of the invisible God and the perfect picture of a faithful human. But most astonishing is that he wants to be in a relationship with you, building into your life and teaching you everything you need to know to become like him. You just need to seek him out and make him your example.

Prayer

Jesus, I want you to be the most important person in my life. Help me to admire you more than I admire my other heroes of the faith. Create in me a strong desire to become like you, choosing faithfulness to my heavenly Father every chance I get. Amen.

31

UNEXPECTED GLORY

Scripture Passage: *"He is the radiance of the glory of God and the exact imprint of his nature, and he upholds the universe by the word of his power."* —Hebrews 1:3

READ: JOHN 1:1–14

I recently hunted elk in Oregon's high desert. Allen, my guide, grew up there and knew the rugged terrain like the back of his weathered hand. He knew where the elk wintered, how to stalk within a few hundred yards of the herd, and which cow calls would seduce the bulls into shooting range. He led me through this wilderness, and I was glad to follow.

But as Allen and I traversed a few hills near camp the first morning, I realized that we were traveling in different gears. He was taking long strides over the rocky terrain with his head down, covering ground quickly. I was meandering, stopping frequently to photograph a rocky crag or enjoy a deep breath of the crisp air scented with sagebrush. At the end of the day, as we sat beside the campfire, I asked Allen, "How can you not be utterly astonished every time you walk in these mountains? You're walking without looking, and I can't take my eyes off the terrain."

He stared at the fire for a moment, then replied, "I guess it's because I grew up here. It's almost too familiar by now."

It can be the same for me with the cornfields, rivers, and woods of Nebraska. I recently took an out-of-state guest to the Platte River near our house; he gasped a sigh of awe when he saw the size of the cottonwood trees by the water. I had long ago stopped noticing those trees. We easily become too familiar with beautiful things. We can even become dulled to the glory of God. "Glory" is a commonly used word in the Bible. To glorify something means to experience or point to the greatness and beauty of that thing.

Mountains have glory. People have glory. The work of our hands has glory. To have glory is to contain power, beauty, and greatness. Of all things containing glory, nothing on earth compares to God. As weighty and wonderful as the mountains of the high desert are, they are limited. Only their Creator has unlimited glory, because only he is infinite in power, beauty, and greatness.

When God took on flesh and dwelt among us, he let us see his glory in a personal way. John 1:14 records, "And the Word became flesh and dwelt among us, and we have seen his glory, glory as of the only Son from the Father, full of grace and truth." Many people missed Jesus's glory entirely. The nation of Israel was waiting for a Messiah, but they thought he would be a powerful king and a mighty warrior who would liberate them from Rome. They expected a man clothed in light, flexing giant spiritual muscles. Instead, God's Son, the Messiah, wore a robe and sandals, spent time with children, beggars, and tax collectors, and liberated people from sin, not political oppression. He wasn't what they were looking for, so many overlooked his glory altogether.

We must allow God to define his glory or we will miss it. The glory of God in Jesus was wrapped in humility, taking on the form of a common, ordinary man who would be rejected, humiliated, and put to death so that we might be saved. His beauty was seen in his meekness and in his gentle, compassionate heart.

Just as the high desert displayed its glory on my elk trip, God loves to show himself to us. But we need to have eyes to see. We must long to see God's beauty, as King David longed to see it when he wrote, "One thing have I asked of the LORD, that will I seek after: that I may dwell in the house of the LORD all the days of my life, to gaze upon the beauty of the LORD and to meditate in his temple" (Ps. 27:4).

Prayer

Jesus, help me see your glory every day. Help me not to miss your beauty because I'm looking for it in seemingly bigger, stronger, more dynamic things. Help me to see your greatness in the way that you loved other people, freed them from their sins, and met their earthly needs. There is none like you, God. Amen.

32

PROVE YOURSELF

Scripture Passage: *"Now to the one who works, his wages are not counted as a gift but as his due. And to the one who does not work but trusts him who justifies the ungodly, his faith is counted as righteousness."* —Romans 4:4–5

READ: 2 CORINTHIANS 5:16–21

Are you the kind of sportsman who tries to impress others with your success? Do you try to catch a bigger fish or shoot a bigger buck than your buddies? Do you have a hard time feeling genuine excitement when someone outdoes you on the water or in the field? If you said yes to any of these questions, you're likely trying to find a sense of significance and acceptance through your performance.

"You need to prove yourself by the things you accomplish" is the message of men's hearts, and it's an idea you find regularly hammered home in our society. In 2010, the Chicago Bears posted a series of videos online that followed rookies from the moment they arrived at training camp through the rigorous tryout process. Eighty players were invited to camp that year. They knew that after a few weeks the coaches would trim that number to sixty-five, and then a few weeks later, when the season started, the roster would be whittled down to fifty-three men.

Rookies knew from day one that there was a good chance they would get cut. One clip captured part of Coach Lovie Smith's orientation talk to the wide-eyed rookies. Looking them in the eyes, he said, "Make us put you on the team."[1]

Coach Smith's message to the rookies was clear, and it is the voice of our culture: "Produce results, or hit the road."

1. "Inside Rookie Minicamp," The Official Website of the Chicago Bears, July 6, 2010, http://www.chicagobears.com/multimedia/.

This message isn't necessarily wrong for an NFL coach to communicate to the men trying out for his team. The sad reality, however, is that as sportsmen, we tend to believe this message, carrying the pressure to prove ourselves into the fields, forests, lakes, and rivers. We love being outside. We love pursuing game. But if we're honest, do we ultimately love the feeling of success more?

The gospel of grace is refreshing because it tells us that we can give up trying to prove ourselves to God once and for all. In fact, the Bible tells us that when we stop looking to our own works and instead believe in a God who forgives sinful people based on faith in Jesus, we gain the acceptance we've always longed for. Romans 4:5 states, "And to the one who does not work but trusts him who justifies the ungodly, his faith is counted as righteousness." This verse is a clear picture of what is required for salvation. Becoming a Christian is not about attending church, cleaning up our act, or taking part in religious rituals. It's about trusting that the life and death of Christ is now ours by faith, and we are perfect now because Jesus is perfect. Jesus makes us significant, valuable, and acceptable to God.

The Christian sportsman doesn't need to wrap a tag around a world-record rack in order to feel like he counts for something. He doesn't have to log a fish into a record book to know he's got what it takes. By faith, he knows that Jesus settled the issue of acceptance once and for all. He's now free to simply enjoy spending time outside chasing game with friends for the love of the sport. The pressure is off.

Prayer

My gracious Father, thank you for the life and death of Jesus and what he accomplished for me. I depend on his perfect life in order to be perfect in your sight. I depend on his death in order to be forgiven and spared your wrath. Please help me quit trying to prove myself by my performance and rather live by grace through faith in Jesus. Amen.

33

RAINY, DAMP
CLOSENESS

Scripture Passage: *"The LORD is a stronghold for the
oppressed, a stronghold in times of trouble."*—Psalm 9:9

READ: PSALM 34:17-22

Seasons are vital. We need times of sunshine and blue skies. We also
need times of rain and clouds. Robert Morgan, in his biography
of Daniel Boone, describes how Boone felt closer to nature when
bad weather rolled in. He writes, "[Boone] may have been one of
those who feel the woods are more alive in the rain, the air more
intimate, immediate with sounds and smells, with moisture and
falling drops. Every sound, every leaf, is vivid."[1]

Daniel Boone's senses were keener on a rainy day. When the
clouds rolled in, he felt the woods come alive. He could see and
smell with greater precision. He expected to encounter more of the
game he pursued—Boone understood that creatures felt safer on
the quiet, water-softened forest carpet. In Boone's opinion, dark
days provided a unique opportunity to experience nature.

The Bible talks about the dark, damp seasons of life in a similar
way. When we're sad or in pain, God offers a unique opportunity to
experience him and sense his presence. Scripture is clear that God
walks closely with those who are suffering. He is a friend to the
lonely, a husband to the widow, and a father to the fatherless. He
is able to relate to our grief and loss in a unique way. As a Father,
he experienced the death of his Son. As a man, he experienced
persecution and rejection from the people he was trying to help.
As a friend, he knew the sadness of saying good-bye for a season.
God shows up in the dark, damp seasons of our lives and he walks

1. Robert Morgan, *Boone: A Biography* (Chapel Hill, NC: Algonquin Books,
2007), 36.

with us: "Even though I walk through the valley of the shadow of death, I will fear no evil, for you are with me" (Ps. 23:4).

When I was in college, one of my close friends committed suicide. Marcus had just finished training to become a Navy Seal when he ended his life. Marcus's death was the most painful thing I had ever experienced. It raised many questions that to this day remain unanswered. But my pain was more than intellectual; it was deeply emotional and relational. I remember spending several nights alone in my dorm room loft, reading the Bible and begging God to comfort Marcus's family. Those were dark, damp nights, but they were some of the richest, most intimate times with the Lord that I've ever known. I sensed God's presence and comfort in a way that I'd never known or needed before.

Thinking back on that difficult period of my life, I am filled with thankfulness and hope. Thankfulness because God proved to me that he walks with those who suffer. Hope because I know that, despite more dark days ahead, his presence will be real and tangible and intimate. That time following Marcus's death reminds me that God will not leave us alone; he shows up in a personal, unique way when we struggle.

Prayer

Father, help me sense your presence during the painful, difficult seasons of life. You are the God of all comfort; please walk with me through the valley of the shadow of death and help me fear no evil. Amen.

34

NEVER WITHOUT

Scripture Passage: *"And God said, 'Behold, I have given you every plant yielding seed that is on the face of all the earth, and every tree with seed in its fruit. You shall have them for food.'"* —Genesis 1:29

READ: MATTHEW 6:25–34

My son, Aidan, snaked his hand through the vines and wire cage to grab the first ripe Brandywine tomato. His arm stretched all the way into the plant, up to his shoulder, as he gently twisted the fruit so as to not damage the vine or its treasure. He pulled the tomato out, hoisted it up for me to see, and we admired the fruit that would soon join onions, peppers, lime juice, and cilantro. Heaven moves just a bit closer to earth when our family enjoys a big bowl of garden-fresh salsa.

There is so much in life to be enjoyed, and often this richness involves land, animals, fruits, and vegetables. I love gardening, hunting, or exploring creation with my children. In fact, my children often help me enjoy these passions. As adults we tend to lose the wonder. We are born into this world of overwhelming gifts and astonishing delights. But by the time we've seen ten thousand sunrises, witnessed a thousand shooting stars, or peeled back our hundredth pomegranate, the shine tends to wear off. The extraordinary becomes ordinary and we start to sleepwalk through this world of divine gifts. But take a child into a garden and watch their fascination with a pumpkin growing perfectly on the vine, and you just might find yourself reawakened from your slumber.

The book of Genesis describes the origins of the earth and all things upon it. But if you go to Genesis simply to answer the "how" questions, you're apt to miss the deeper purpose of the text. The author of Genesis is primarily concerned with showing us *why* God created the world the way he did. For example, Genesis 1:29 shows us we were created to need food and to see God as our provider.

I live in a farming community in Nebraska. Hardworking men and women live with dirt underneath their fingernails year-round in order to bring in a crop. But at the same time, these farmers recognize their dependence upon God's creation and his active provision for the success of their crops. Farmers, more than many, understand that God is the source of life. Every year they place dormant seeds in the nutrient-rich soil and then pray and wait for God to give the seeds life and growth.

The same goes for God's provision through fishing and hunting. It's hard for me to spend a day on the water, or to walk fields for pheasant, without appreciating the ways that God caused his world to yield delicious and satisfying food. The other day my son and I caught a creel full of trout from Pine Creek in northern Nebraska. That night, as we fried the fish in sea salt, black pepper, and butter made from fresh milk, we gave thanks. When we understand how God has created us, provided for us, and delighted us, we can only give thanks. No other response will do.

Prayer

Father, open my eyes to enjoy and appreciate all the ways you provide for me each day. You are so good, and your care toward me is greater than your care toward the grass of the field or the birds of the air. I praise you on this day that you have made. Amen.

35

Unstoppable

Scripture Passage: *"Whatever the LORD pleases, he does, in heaven and on earth, in the seas and all deeps."*
—Psalm 135:6

READ: DANIEL 4:34–35

The felt soles on my boots didn't hold. As I stepped from rock to rock, my foot slipped on moss and I fell into a deep hole in the river. Cold water spilled over the top of my waders, down my pants, and into my right boot. I grabbed a clump of grass on the bank, righted myself, and then went back to fly-fishing. Twenty minutes later, I caught a fifteen-inch rainbow trout on a copper-headed nymph. It didn't matter that my wool socks were wet and cold—I was warm and alive inside.

Few things exhilarate me more than a raging river, a rocky crag, or a forest full of pine trees. Aldo Leopold captures my heart perfectly: "There are some who can live without wild things, and some who cannot. These essays are the delights and dilemmas of one who cannot."[1]

Like Leopold, I cannot live without wild things. This is one reason I'm so attracted to the God of the Bible. I will never encounter anything or anyone more untamable than God. To be wild means to not be limited or restrained. Something that is wild does not answer to us, is not controlled by human hands. It is highly unpredictable and cannot be made to carry out our will. These are the qualities of wild things, and these are the qualities of our Creator. Nebuchadnezzar, the Babylonian king whom God humbled, declared, "All the inhabitants of the earth are accounted as nothing, and he does according to his will among the host of heaven and

1. Aldo Leopold, *A Sand County Almanac: With Essays on Conservation* (New York: Oxford University Press, 1949), 21.

among the inhabitants of the earth; and none can stay his hand or say to him, 'What have you done?'" (Dan. 4:35). No one can stop God's hand. No one can question him about the things he does. No one can tame God.

But that doesn't seem to stop us from trying. Sermons are preached and books are written that attempt to reduce God to a formula. We try to make God predictable, suggesting that he will respond to us in certain ways when we carry out certain behaviors. We apply this formulaic approach to God in numerous categories, but let's look at parenting as an example.

We often think the formula for God doing what we want with our children looks something like this: I pray + read the Scriptures + discipline + read the latest parenting book and follow its advice = God will give me a child who is well behaved and faithful. When we think of God in this manner, in parenting or any other area of life, we reveal our desire to domesticate the most untamable Being in our lives.

The Creator of all things doesn't fit into our linear equations for him, and thank God that he doesn't. His powerful and unpredictable nature ought to humble and invigorate us. When I was navigating rocks and currents in order to angle for trout, I was reminded that I was not the most powerful force in that environment. The river was bigger and stronger than me, and I was not in control of it in any way. These qualities are precisely why I go to this river—they infuse me with life and remind me how important it is to feel small and vulnerable at times. This is what a right understanding about the untamable nature of God does for us. It keeps us on our toes and in awe of the God we can't predict.

Prayer

God, you are in control and I am not. Help my heart to be appropriately humbled by your greatness and majesty. Help me not to domesticate you or try to make you predictable. Keep me in awe of your supreme power over all created things. Amen.

36

DON'T BLINK

Scripture Passage: *"And rising very early in the morning, while it was still dark, he departed and went out to a desolate place, and there he prayed."* —Mark 1:35

READ: PSALM 119:89-104

My wife's parents, Bev and RB, visited us in the hospital after Jamie gave birth to our first child, Kate. We spent several hours together as a family, laughing, crying, and doting over our beautiful little girl. When the time came for them to leave, RB paused at the door, walked back over to Jamie's hospital bed, and rubbed Kate's head. Tears pooled in his eyes. He picked up his hand from Kate's head and put it on Jamie's hand. He gazed at us with a look of total sincerity and said, "Don't blink . . . it goes by so fast."

Most of us are tired. But more than that, we're tired of being tired. We are fed up with the sense that life is speeding by and we're missing most of it. We want to be able to spend time outside, or at the dinner table, or playing catch with our children. And we don't want to just live through those moments but to know that we are fully engaging in them. We want to appreciate everything and not miss anything.

When Jesus pulled away from the crowd to spend time alone with his Father, he modeled an important aspect of living a meaningful, "don't blink" life. Jesus had a demanding schedule; everywhere he went, people wanted things from him. The crowds wanted him to preach, heal the sick, and cast out demons. The religious leaders wanted him to perform miracles. Even his own disciples wanted him to explain everything he did for everyone else. He was always on call, always in demand, and always fielding requests. This rabbi from Nazareth spent almost all of his time with people. *Almost* all. Mark 1:35 shows us that Jesus made sure he had time alone with his Father to pray, reflect, and examine his life. Spending time alone with God was an essential part of Jesus's strategy for living well.

This idea can feel counterintuitive. We are in the habit of rushing from one thing to the next, adding stress to stress, chaos to chaos, and complexity to complexity. We wear out our shoes at an alarming pace, and it keeps us from living thoughtful, reflective, intentional lives. Socrates once said, "The unexamined life is not worth living." We can work, play, and even do ministry so hard for so long that we feel distanced from God and detached from the most important people in our lives. Part of running hard involves resting easy, and we need time alone with God to experience and enjoy this rest.

As sportsmen, we often spend time away from people, in God's creation, with room to breathe and think. Several years ago, RB, the same man who warned me not to blink, modeled a strategy for making the most of my times afield. RB was preparing for a whitetail hunt to Canada, and before he left, he asked everyone in the family to write down their prayer requests so he could pray for them while he was in the stand. He also copied Scripture onto note cards, thinking in advance about passages he wanted to consider more deeply. My father-in-law ended up shooting a giant whitetail with chocolate-colored antlers, but his favorite part of the trip was the time he spent with the Lord reflecting on his life and praying for his family and friends. He came home refreshed and ready to run back into his demanding schedule.

These pleasures are available for each of us. We just need to spend time each day with the Lord, in his Word, listening to his voice. Life flies by quickly. But when we make quiet, intentional time with our Savior a priority, we won't miss a thing.

Prayer

Father, help me add this aspect of intentionality to my times hunting and fishing. You have given me a busy, active life, and I want to make the most of it. Help me enjoy my times alone with you so that when I return to my work and relationships, I am refreshed, renewed, and ready to run again. Amen.

37

THE INTEGRATED LIFE

Scripture Passage: *"So, whether you eat or drink, or whatever you do, do all to the glory of God."* —1 Corinthians 10:31

READ: COLOSSIANS 3:12-17

I was in a bear hunting camp for a week with four other men. The oldest, Dave, was sharp-tongued. He spit out racist and sexist jokes all week long. On Sunday morning, we had a mini church service in camp. When we asked if anyone would like to close in prayer, Dave unexpectedly volunteered. His praise to God flowed like milk and honey from his lips; he knew the words to say and the cadence with which to say them. A few quick moments after he said amen, he was back to telling his jokes.

A faithful Christian must learn to live an integrated life. Many of us divide life into two categories: the secular (activities without God) and the sacred (activities with God). For Dave, church was sacred but the rest of life was secular. This fractured, compartmentalized view of life is not biblical. The Bible tells us that when we trust in Jesus, the Spirit of God enters our lives and dwells within us at all times. "And by this we know that he abides in us, by the Spirit whom he has given us" (1 John 3:24). Where God is, life is sacred. And for the believer, God is always present.

Our sense of nearness to God suffers when we fail to see all of life as sacred. If certain activities seem "secular" to us, we will carry them out without feeling close to Jesus, as if he is not with us in the moment. We may rush through those activities and try not to think about God, or perhaps we apologize to God for how we have "wasted" our time. Tragically, we think God is not with us in those "secular" moments. The reality is that God is with us at all times, and there isn't a moment in our lives when we need to shut him out or pretend he's not watching. Paul chose eating and drinking as examples of activities we can do for Jesus. If something as everyday and mundane as eating and drinking can be done with God for his glory, then nothing is secular. Everything is sacred.

If we believe and practice this truth, it will radically change our lives. Sin will feel grossly inappropriate . . . because God is with us. Seemingly ordinary tasks will become eternally significant . . . because God is with us. And times when we feel lonely, isolated, or apart from God will become times of rich communion with our Creator . . . because God is with us. Whether we are sitting in church singing worship songs or telling jokes around a campfire, we will know God is with us and that we're in a sacred place taking part in sacred activities.

Prayer

Holy Spirit, thank you for being with me at all times. Help me to fully comprehend that I am living every moment with the Lord. And help that reality shape the way I think, feel, speak, and act. May all my life be lived for your glory, God. Amen.

38

Acting Like Men

Scripture Passage: *"Be watchful, stand firm in the faith, act like men, be strong. Let all that you do be done in love."*
—1 Corinthians 16:13–14

READ: DEUTERONOMY 31:6–8

I once saw a man wrap a shotgun barrel around a fence post. I had taken a few of my co-workers to eastern Nebraska to hunt pheasants on my uncle's farm. Joe, the man who destroyed the gun, had brought his thirteen-year-old son along with him. His son had been posted at the end of a field when a rooster flushed and flew his direction. He shot at the bird and his pellets spread out, spraying the milo field and the men walking toward him. A few pieces of lead hit Joe in the face, and in a rage, he ran up to his son, took the Remington 870 Express from his hands, and swung it like a baseball bat against a nearby fence post. The stock shattered and the barrel bent. The gun was permanently damaged in that moment. So was his son.

All boys grow up trying to understand masculinity. What makes a man a man? Unfortunately, our culture tends to suggest that manhood is about acquiring power, job titles, authority, and the ability to earn money. Young boys who take their cue from culture grow up viewing masculinity as loud, assertive, and oftentimes abrasive behavior. And they often grow up with the capacity to wrap shotguns around fence posts.

The Scriptures cast a different vision of masculinity. According to the Bible, a masculine man guards and protects the hearts, welfare, and needs of those who are weak. He uses his physical strength, his voice, and his stature to shield the young, the old, the powerless, and the vulnerable from evil or harm. He teaches with kindness and patience, not with temper and threats. And he doesn't attempt to prove his significance or manhood by how much he owns, what titles or degrees he has behind his name, or by how much he can lift. He proves his masculinity by his generosity, as Isaiah 58:6–7 instructs:

> Is not this the fast that I choose: to loose the bonds of wickedness, to undo the straps of the yoke, to let the oppressed go free, and to break every yoke? Is it not to share your bread with the hungry and bring the homeless poor into your house; when you see the naked, to cover him, and not to hide yourself from your own flesh?

I want to be masculine as the Word of God defines the character of a man. Gentle. Strong. Kind. Generous. Faithful. Hardworking. Honest. Protective. Loyal. These are a few of the qualities that will characterize a man of God. Men who exhibit these traits are a tremendous force for good. People know when they are in the presence of masculinity. Biblical manhood bears a distinctive fruit.

Prayer

Father, I want to be a truly masculine man, and I need your help. By your Spirit, give me a new vision for what it means to serve and protect those in my life. Help me to seek out opportunities to be generous and kind, not greedy and self-serving. Help my picture of manhood to be defined by your Word, not by culture. Amen.

39

NEVER SHOW
YOUR NECK

Scripture Passage: *"And he said to them, 'Take care, and be on your guard against all covetousness, for one's life does not consist in the abundance of his possessions.'"*—Luke 12:15

READ: 1 JOHN 2:15–17

A landowner a half mile from our house recently captured footage of a mountain lion on a trail camera. This was sober news. A mountain lion takes down its prey by sneaking from behind, leaping onto its victim, and clamping down on its neck. By the time a deer, dog, or human realizes what has happened, it's incapacitated, its spinal column severed.

To escape a mountain lion, you need to see it, and you need to face it eye to eye. Author Craig Childs recalled a memorable experience he had with such a beast: "The mountain lion begins to move to my left, and I turn, keeping my face on it, my knife at my right side. It paces to my right, trying to get around on my other side, to get behind me. I turn right, staring at it . . . my stare is about the only defense I have."[1] This staring match between cat and man continued for several tense moments before the lion wandered back into the woods. Childs won the standoff by taking the threat seriously and by not showing his neck.

When Jesus warns us about money and the feelings of greed and covetousness it produces, he uses mountain lion–defense language. He says, "Take care, and be on your guard" (Luke 12:15). The human heart longs to possess things. We think that if we have "one more thing," or if we could just have the item that the person next to us has, then we will be happy and satisfied.

1. Craig Childs, *The Animal Dialogues: Uncommon Encounters in the Wild* (New York: Back Bay Books, 2007), 64.

IN PURSUIT

I watched a child in our church nursery pick up and discard a stuffed panda. The same child went bonkers two minutes later when another little boy picked up the same panda and began playing with it. The fuzzy critter didn't hold any appeal until his friend possessed it.

Jesus warns us to recognize this threat of envy and greed, and to never expose our necks to it. If we sense ourselves longing for a new bow like our hunting buddy's, or a boat as nice as the one downriver, we need to recognize that these feelings are some of the great predators of our hearts. When we recognize them as our foe, we are able to take them to God and ask him to help us overcome them.

One of my friends recently purchased a new rifle. As he was sharing the news with me, my mind started scheming ways that I could buy the same gun. In that moment, I realized what I was doing, and I prayed and asked God to help me be content with the gun I already owned. Like Craig Childs in his moment of victory, I felt a great sense of relief wash over me. If we take the threat of covetousness seriously, face it eye to eye, and ask God to protect our necks, he will help us escape.

Prayer

Lord, I know that I will be happier in life when I learn to be content with what I have—please help me have this sense of contentment. Help me to lay up treasures in heaven and not store up stuff here on earth. Help me recognize when my heart is coveting something someone else has, and then help me escape those beastly feelings. Amen.

40

Good with Words

Scripture Passage: *"If you abide in me, and my words abide in you, ask whatever you wish, and it will be done for you."* —John 15:7

Read: Romans 8:26–30

I'm not adept at prayer. Just the other day, an older sportsman in our church stopped by my office to chat. It was the six-month anniversary of his wife's death, and he wanted to pray with a friend. He sat quietly on the chair next to me as I spoke with God about comfort, encouragement, and friendship. I felt clumsy with my words and knew that I hadn't communicated exactly what was going on inside.

I've found that most men talk with God every day, yet rarely feel like they are able to say exactly what's on their mind and heart. We tend to feel things deeply, but we have a difficult time verbalizing these feelings and concerns. Even when we are able to sort out what's going on inside, it's hard to find the words to communicate it. It's one thing to shake another man's hand, look him in the eye, and talk about work or the weather. It's something entirely different to speak with our Creator, whom we cannot see, about the deepest issues of the heart.

A few days ago, I took a list of prayer items to the field with me. Before I left the house, I talked with Jamie about the names and situations with ease and heartfelt concern. Yet, when I got to the stand and started to talk with God, my tongue twisted in knots and I couldn't express myself with the same ease and comfort.

This struggle with prayer once bothered me, but now I'm no longer discouraged or frustrated. The breakthrough happened when I studied Romans 8:26–27, where it is revealed that the Spirit of God helps me communicate with God by interceding for me "with groanings too deep for words." I don't always know what to say, but that's okay—the Holy Spirit knows my heart and knows how to communicate it for me. He keeps me connected to my Father in heaven at all times. Even when I'm struggling with words, he always knows what to say.

God doesn't demand that you say the right things or talk a certain amount of time in order to stay in his good graces. If you've trusted in Jesus for salvation, God is as pleased with you as he possibly can be, and mastering the art of prayer isn't going to earn you any favor or merit in his eyes. Instead, he wants you to know that he understands your weaknesses and struggles, and loves you in spite of them. In fact, he sent his Spirit to dwell in you so that you always have fellowship and intimacy with God. Your prayers are perfect, whether they sound polished to you or not. You can, as Paul said, "pray without ceasing" (1 Thess. 5:17) and know that, thanks to God, you're always good with words.

Prayer

Father, thank you for the amazing gift of your Spirit. Thank you for helping me in my weaknesses, even my weakness to communicate what is on my heart and mind. Help me feel loved and accepted by you so that I feel unhindered in my prayers. Help me to know you are with me at all times so that I desire to pray without ceasing. Amen.

41

REBUILDING
BROKEN MEN

Scripture Passage: *"But this is the one to whom I will look: he who is humble and contrite in spirit and trembles at my word."* —Isaiah 66:2

READ: 2 CHRONICLES 7:11-22

I drove a 1975 Chrysler Cordoba when I was in college. I bought it for $1,500 in 1989, and a full tank would get me to my favorite fishing spot and back. Three years after I bought the 'Doba, the engine started clanking. At first, the sound was barely perceptible and only showed up when I drove long distances. But it soon became louder and more frequent. I was a senior, dining nightly on Ramen noodles and diced-up hot dogs. Naturally, I didn't have an auto repair fund. But I did have a strategy for dealing with the problem: as the noise grew louder and louder, I turned my radio up higher and higher. It's amazing how much you can't hear when the dial is cranked all the way.

Shockingly, my strategy didn't work for very long. Two months before graduation, I was parked at a four-way stoplight in the middle of Lincoln, fishing poles sticking out the back window, when dark smoke started billowing from under the hood. Now I needed the radio to drown out the honking coming from behind me.

Many men are hearing internal clanking noises, but they've turned up the volume by increasing their activities—hobbies, work, and sports. They're racing from one thing to another, leaking smoke from all sides of the hood. The breakdown is happening in our hearts, the private world no one else can see. We fill our schedules, hoping to silence our inner lives.

God cautions us to pay attention to our heart in Proverbs 4:23: "Keep your heart with all vigilance, for from it flow the springs of life." What does it mean to "keep your heart" so that you experience life, peace, and joy? Scripture actually has much to say about this. We must protect our hearts from sin, as Colossians 3:5 tells us: "Put to death therefore what is earthly in you: sexual immorality, impurity, passion, evil desire, and covetousness, which is idolatry." Recognizing sinful desires, confessing them, and choosing not to engage in them are key to guarding our hearts.

Perhaps the most important step we can take is asking God for help. Only he can give us the wisdom to identify what's broken. And only God can fix what we find in disrepair. Jeremiah 17:9 says, "The heart is deceitful above all things, and desperately sick; who can understand it?" No person has the ability to diagnose and heal his own heart problems. But God can. In the next verse, God says: "I the LORD search the heart and test the mind" (Jer. 17:10). Men can live with passion and zeal when their hearts are healthy. The first step is to pop the hood and, with God's help, take a look inside.

Prayer

Father, help me run with zeal and energy into all my pursuits, but with a healthy heart. Lord, search my heart and help me see if there is anything hurtful or damaged. Then, please help me to heal. Help me lean on you through the rebuilding process, knowing that only you can search, diagnose, and restore heart issues. Amen.

42

BREATHTAKING

Scripture Passage: *"Great is the LORD, and greatly to
be praised, and his greatness is unsearchable."* —Psalm
145:3

READ: PSALM 96

Iconic fisherman Izaak Walton wrote about the "various beauties"
of the natural world: "And for the most of them, because they be
so common, most men forget to pay their praises; but let us not;
because it is a sacrifice so pleasing to him that made that sun, and
us, and still protects us, and gives us flowers, and showers, and
stomachs, and meat, and content, and leisure to go a-fishing."[1]
These are strong, beautiful, and apt words about our Creator. And
it pleases God to hear such praise. When the apostle Paul describes
why God chose us and gave us every spiritual blessing in the heav-
ens, he tells us God did this so we might praise his glorious grace
(Eph. 1:6). God loves to delight us to the point where we can't
help but tell of his goodness.

Some people recoil at the idea that God gave us life and placed
us in this world so we would praise him. I spoke about this at a
sportsmen's banquet once. After the event, I approached a man who
had been sitting in the back of the room with his arms crossed and
a look of disgust on his face. When I asked him what he thought
of the message, he replied, "So, God made us to praise him? That
seems egotistical, like one of those showboating football players
who does a victory dance after a touchdown. I hate those guys!"

Those guys get on my nerves, too. There's something silly and
inappropriate when a flawed, finite person expects other people to
sing his praises. And who isn't in that category of "flawed"? The

1. Izaak Walton, *The Complete Angler* (New York: Macmillan, 1901), 174.

best wide receiver in the NFL may make an outstanding catch on one down, only to drop the ball on the next. Even in our best moments, we lack complete goodness, beauty, and virtue. But God is not like us. He is infinitely good, beautiful, and virtuous. When we praise him, we are doing what is most appropriate. He deserves it, and we benefit from it.

When we direct our appreciation toward something that is *truly* worthy, we experience pleasure from the act of praise. For example, it feels good to savor and celebrate a tender, juicy prime rib. Admiring a snowcapped mountain range or a beautiful sunset is meaningful. And it is rewarding to celebrate a lifelong friend for his loyalty. We are singing praises in all three examples and finding great pleasure and happiness in doing so. Why? Because these objects are worthy of our praise, and to praise worthy objects is pleasurable.

Likewise, God is worthy, infinitely worthy. He is immeasurably powerful, lovely, mysterious, wild, and alluring. He is the embodiment and definition of majesty and power. Everything we see in nature that is rugged or breathtakingly beautiful reflects God's creative mind. The fact that God chose us and gave us grace that we might praise him is a tremendous gift to us. We get to enjoy his grace. We also get to enjoy praising him for it.

Prayer

Lord, I cannot find the words to express how great you are. You are worthy of all my praise and adoration, and I give it to you with all my heart. Help me see you as the most praiseworthy person in my life. Give me a heart that is filled with joy because it recognizes your power, beauty, and perfection. Amen.

43

An Audience of One

Scripture Passage: *"And no creature is hidden from his sight, but all are naked and exposed to the eyes of him to whom we must give account."* —Hebrews 4:13

Read: Daniel 6

All three of us jumped. My ten-year-old son, Aidan, squeezed my pant leg. We were standing on a driveway and talking to Mike, the landowner, when a gunshot interrupted the peaceful, crisp night air. The blast came from the gravel road about a half mile from Mike's house. The gunshot was out of place, and it startled us. The sun had been down about an hour, and the night was black as coal. I left Aidan with Mike, jumped into my pickup, and sped off to confront the shooter. The moment my headlights lit up the road, I saw another set of lights come on and a truck raced away. The encounter was over in a moment, but the bad taste in my mouth lingered.

Integrity is best measured when you're alone and you think nobody is watching. Integrity is demonstrated through our consistent thoughts, attitudes, actions, and values. Rock-solid integrity is empowered by faith in a powerful, all-knowing God. Take Daniel for example. He had been captured by the armies of Babylon and was living as a foreigner in a distant land. Because of his wisdom and work ethic, he had risen to a place of prominence in the Babylonian dynasty, capturing the admiration of King Darius. The other aspiring leaders of Babylon hated him for it, so they scrutinized Daniel's life, looking for anything negative or shameful they could exploit and taint the king's affection. They found nothing. Daniel 6:4 records, "Then the high officials and the satraps sought to find a ground for complaint against Daniel with regard to the kingdom, but they could find no ground for complaint or any fault, because he was faithful, and no error or fault was found in him."

Can you imagine having an entire group of ambitious, intelligent leaders investigating your life in order to find any flaw or sin? The reason that Daniel held up under such vigorous scrutiny was that he was full of faith. Verse 4 tells us that they couldn't find anything "because he was faithful."

Many people can claim knowledge of God and confidently state that they have biblical values. But there is a difference between consenting to truth and believing in the presence of God. The secret to Daniel's integrity was knowing God was with him at all times, and this knowledge impacted his reality. Daniel knew that, whether he was alone in the dark or standing by the king's side in front of the entire nation of Babylon, his primary audience was God. He didn't live to please the king. He didn't live to please his co-workers. He didn't even live to please himself. Daniel had an audience of one, and this motivated him to make wise, honorable choices.

Most sportsmen would say that they want to have true integrity. The secret is having a heart full of faith, trusting that God is always present and active in our lives. Hudson Taylor, the courageous missionary to China, said it this way, "All God's giants have been weak men, who did great things for God because they reckoned on his being with them."[1] When we know God is with us, we act like God is with us. That's faith-driven integrity.

Prayer

Father, give me a faith in you so strong and deep that it causes me to make good, honorable choices no matter who is watching. Help me know that you are with me at all times. I desire to be a man of integrity, but I want that godly character to be fueled and impassioned by my faith in you, the living God. Amen.

1. Dr. and Mrs. Howard Taylor, *The Biography of James Hudson Taylor* (London: China Inland Mission, 1965), 316.

44

Baiting Others' Hooks

Scripture Passage: *"In all things I have shown you that by working hard in this way we must help the weak and remember the words of the Lord Jesus, how he himself said, 'It is more blessed to give than to receive.'"* —Acts 20:35

Read: Mark 10:35–45

When I was around five years old, my mom would sometimes say, "Let's go fishing, Son! I'll bet they're biting today."

Then we would fish together, which actually meant that for two hours she would untangle my line, bait my hook, and celebrate every tiny bluegill I hauled in. Rarely did I see my mom cast her line in the water during those early childhood times of fishing together. She was too busy helping me find success.

Our culture appropriately places a high emphasis on leading by being out in front. But we often fail to recognize the equally important priority of leading by serving other people. To serve is to work toward another person's benefit. The Bible tells us to serve the Lord: "Do not be slothful in zeal, be fervent in spirit, serve the Lord" (Rom. 12:11). It also tells us to serve one another: "For you were called to freedom, brothers. Only do not use your freedom as an opportunity for the flesh, but through love serve one another. For the whole law is fulfilled in one word: 'You shall love your neighbor as yourself'" (Gal. 5:13–14).

Jesus is the perfect example of service. Nobody was worthy of more respect and honor than Jesus, and his disciples understood this. In fact, they understood this so well that they didn't question that Jesus would be the most important person in eternity. They argued about which of them would get to be in the second highest position of honor. James and John even asked for these positions of leadership and glory: "Grant us to sit, one at your right hand and one at your left, in your glory" (Mark 10:37).

We tend to feel shocked and righteously indignant at this request, but it's a demand very much in line with how this world thinks about leadership and performance: those who have worked the hardest and displayed the most loyalty deserve the greatest honor, highest salaries, and most prestigious positions. Presidents promote loyal cabinet workers. Head coaches promote faithful position coaches. Bosses promote trustworthy employees. It's how things are done here on earth. James and John were simply asking for the status quo of this performance-based world.

But the status quo in this world is not the status quo in the kingdom of God. Jesus responds to James and John by flipping the world's system upside down. He says, "But whoever would want to be great among you must be your servant, and whoever would be first among you must be slave of all" (Mark 10:43–44). And then, in a shocking turn of events, Jesus uses himself as the example in verse 45: "For even the Son of Man came not to be served but to serve, and to give his life as a ransom for many."

The sportsman who lives in the kingdom of God measures greatness not by who shoots the largest elk or catches the longest northern pike but rather by who earnestly desires other people's success and welfare. My mother felt more personal satisfaction when I caught a fish than when her own bobber went under. That's the heart of a servant. That's the heart of true leadership.

Prayer

Jesus, help me live according to the values of the kingdom of God and not the kingdom of this world. Help me to lead by serving those in my life, not by expecting them to serve me. Jesus, thank you for your humility and example of servant leadership. Help me to be like you. Amen.

45

GOD'S WOODSHED

Scripture Passage: *"If you are left without discipline, in which all have participated, then you are illegitimate children and not sons."*—Hebrews 12:8

READ: REVELATION 3:19–22

I didn't chastise my friend's son, although he certainly needed some gentle correction. Jon and I were setting up archery targets for a 3D shoot, and his son was following behind us and knocking them down. Jon had asked his son a couple times to stop, but the little guy was in an ornery mood. I care about Jon's son, and so I encouraged him to obey his father. But that's as far as I went. I didn't think that it was my place to chastise my friend's child.

I do, however, discipline my own children. What's the difference? I feel a deep sense of fatherly love and concern for Kate, Aidan, and Claire. If they cross lines or endanger themselves or others, I love them enough to carry out consequences. Nobody in the world cares about our children's welfare more than Jamie and me. Our joy is tied to their growth and maturity, so I want them to learn from their mistakes in order to grow up to be wise, thoughtful adults. My discipline, then, flows from my love as a father.

The same is true for us as Christians when it comes to our heavenly Father. He loves us enough to take us to the woodshed when we sin, and this discipline proves his love and concern toward us. God's correction often takes the form of some type of pain or discomfort. It might come through disaster, sickness, or loss. It may also come through the natural consequences of our sins, such as a car accident from drunk driving or getting fired for stealing from our employer.

A man in our community was arrested for possession of an illegal drug with intent to sell. Tom was at church when the police showed up, issued an arrest warrant, and hauled him off to jail. That moment devastated Tom's wife and children and hurt many people in our community. But it also helped change his future. Tom knew that God was good and that God was allowing this consequence into his life for his growth. And Tom *did* grow from that experience, which occurred about six years ago. He now leads an effective ministry to people battling various addictions.

Discipline is rarely fun, but because we can be selfish and immature, it is a vital part of God's plan to lovingly change us into the image of his Son. Our part in the discipline is to recognize the hand of God and remain teachable before him. If we're open to learn, God is always eager to teach.

My friend Jon gave his son a warning, and then when his son knocked down the next target, he turned to me, smiled, and said, "We'll be back in a few minutes." He gently picked up his son and carried him inside. A few moments later, the two of them returned, and they were smiling. Jon's correction, while no doubt uncomfortable for both of them, proved to his son that he cares about his obedience and character. That's the heart of a father.

Prayer

Father, thank you for noticing when I cross lines and do things that are hurtful to myself and others. Thank you for the discipline you bring to my life, as painful as it might feel at the time. I would rather be disciplined by you as your son than be outside your family and fatherly concern for me. Amen.

46

The Thrill in the Ascent

Scripture Passage: *"And I will give you a new heart, and a new spirit I will put within you. And I will remove the heart of stone from your flesh and give you a heart of flesh."* —Ezekiel 36:26

Read: Romans 6:1–4

If you drove me to the base of Mount Everest and told me to climb to the summit, I'd probably find a large, comfortable rock to sit on while I waited for the next bus back to Kathmandu. My lack of motivation would be because I'm painfully aware that I don't have the physical strength, technical skills, or lung capacity to make it to the top. I know I don't have what it takes, so I'd quit before the journey began.

When it comes to pursuing Christlikeness, many men quit before they start. They don't read their Bibles, pray, or seek to grow spiritually, and it's often because they don't think they have what it takes to live the Christian life. As a pastor, I meet with men all the time who are acutely aware that they fall short of God's standards—they know the darkness of their thoughts, the selfishness of their actions, and the things they do when no one is around. They know better than anyone that they are not holy like God is holy, so they call it quits before starting to climb.

God, in his infinite grace, will take us as we are—sins and all—and grow us into men of faith and godly character.

The Bible is full of flawed, sinful people who walked with God by grace and were changed. God took Abraham—a man who had sex with a concubine because he couldn't wait for God to fulfill his promise to him—and made him the father of many nations and kings. God formed David—a man who had a one-night stand with

Bathsheba and then orchestrated her husband's death—into one of the greatest kings of all time. And God took Paul—one of the most bloodthirsty terrorists of the early Christian church—and gave him a new heart, a vibrant faith in Jesus, and an effective ministry to the lost.

The Scriptures are full of "turnarounds"—stories of how God transformed flawed, sinful, screwed-up people into warriors of faith. As Ignatius said, "God uses crooked sticks to draw straight lines." You don't have to be perfect to be a Christian. You just have to get going and trust God will be with you on the journey.

Let us not be timid about knowing God and pursuing his holiness. We are all a long way off. We always will be. God knows this, but he still loves us and invites us to walk with him. We were made for the adventure of knowing God. There's no joy in pouting on a boulder at the base of a mountain just calling out to be climbed. The thrill is in the ascent.

Prayer

Father, I don't want to be a passive bystander in the Christian life. Give me the courage of heart to strike out on this journey of becoming more like you. Help me to walk by your grace and not by my performance. I want to become the man you want me to be. Help me to jump into the journey. Amen.

47

DYING TO LIVE

Scripture Passage: *"If anyone would come after me, let him deny himself and take up his cross daily and follow me."* —Luke 9:23

READ: JOHN 12:20–26

Sometimes it takes a fresh set of eyes to help you see things anew. One October morning, it was James's twelve-year-old eyes that reopened mine. James's dad, Mark, had asked me to take his son hunting. At 9:15 in the morning, as James and I drank hot chocolate and snacked on Pop Tarts, six does popped out of the woods and walked toward our blind. When the lead doe was framed in my shooting window, I pulled back my bow and slipped an arrow behind her front leg. It was a good shot, and the six deer ran about seventy yards before our doe wobbled and fell over into the switchgrass.

"James, we did it! Did you see everything, buddy?"

There was no reply. James sat on his stool, mouth open, staring through his window at the five deer standing beside the dead doe. After several moments of silence, he asked, "Do you think deer feel sad, Zeke?"

James expressed something that we all feel: death is difficult. It takes us aback. This can be one of the hard-to-swallow aspects to the Christian worldview—we preach, sing about, and celebrate the moment a man died on a Roman cross just outside the city gates of Jerusalem. In the Roman Empire, the cross was a horrific instrument of death. We make crosses out of silver and gold and wear them around our necks, but if we could examine the wood of a Roman cross, we would see deep stains of blood and dried flecks of human flesh. And if we could transport ourselves back two thousand years to that fateful moment, we would see absolute horror and despair on the faces of those who loved Jesus.

Because of the horrific, unnatural reality of death, Jesus's command to "take up our cross" is one of the most challenging instructions we will ever receive. Taking up our cross involves putting our self—our desire to find significance, self-worth, and acceptance in the things we accomplish—to death. The man who takes up his cross places Jesus at the center of his affections and makes Jesus, not him*self*, the most important person. Jesus calls the shots from now on. As Dallas Willard wrote, "Being dead to self is the condition where the mere fact that I do not get what I want does not surprise or offend me and has no control over me."[1] We don't fight, work, or strive to get what we want anymore, because we now live for what God wants. Our flesh and its self-importance are now dead, and our heart is now alive to think of God's kingship and kingdom.

We die to self, not as a morbid act of self-abasement, but as an act of life-giving faith. We do it because we believe that, as kernels of corn sprout into new life when they are placed in the ground, we too will truly live once we die to self and follow Christ. And live not just now but for all eternity. For Jesus promised, "Whoever loves his life loses it, and whoever hates his life in this world will keep it for eternal life" (John 12:25).

Prayer

Jesus, help me die to self in order that I might truly live in you. I'm tired of being at the center of my life, trying to control and orchestrate everything to advance my own goals for myself. I want to advance you and your cause, Jesus. Help me to surrender my life and live for your glory. I know that is where I'll find true joy. Amen.

1. Dallas Willard, *Renovation of the Heart: Putting on the Character of Christ* (Colorado Springs: NavPress, 2002), 71.

48

DEER POSING AS ELK

Scripture Passage: *"A new commandment I give to you, that you love one another: just as I have loved you, you also are to love one another. By this all people will know that you are my disciples, if you have love for one another."* —John 13:34–35

READ: 1 CORINTHIANS 13

When I think of an elk, I envision branching tines majestically threading through pine trees. When I think of a pheasant, I imagine copper-colored feathers, a bright red neckband offset starkly by white, and a daggerlike tail feather. And when I think of a tom turkey, I see a beard as fat as a paintbrush dragging on the ground. These are the distinguishing marks of these extraordinary creatures.

A Christian has a distinguishing mark as well: the love he shows to other people. Francis Schaeffer writes, "The world has a right to look upon us as we, as true Christians, come to practical differences and it should be able to observe that we do love each other. Our love must have a form that the world must observe, it must be seeable."[1] A "seeable" love for others motivated by Jesus Christ is what sets a Christian man apart from other men.

Two years ago, a man in our small town left his wife and four-year-old son for a younger woman. When I went to visit the single mom and her child, they were wrapped up together in a blanket on the couch, crying. This woman was forced to put her son in day care and to figure out how to pay the bills, make the meals, and maintain her car, house, and finances. Word of this crisis spread quickly, and four men from our church raced to the desperate mother's side. They didn't offer to help; they simply showed up at

1. Francis A. Schaeffer, *The Mark of the Christian*, 2nd ed. (Downers Grove, IL: InterVarsity, 2006), 58.

her house, sleeves already rolled up, and got to work. For months these four modern-day knights mowed her lawn, changed the oil in her car, and took her son fishing and hunting.

These men did all this work quietly, not wanting to draw attention to themselves or this woman's situation. But in a town the size of Central City, Nebraska, people notice. The way these men served this family was the talk of the town at the pancake house, hardware store, and local garage. People were stunned by how loving and other-centered these men were during this time of need. As their pastor, I kept fielding questions such as, "What's up with these men?" or "What would cause these guys to help someone they barely know?"

My answer was always the same: "That's what *Christian* men do. It's their mark."

A deer can wander the Rocky Mountains claiming to be a bull elk. He can stick out his chest, walk in a dominant fashion, and try his hardest to bugle into the valleys. But to everyone who sees him, he's simply a deer. He lacks the mark of the elk, the majestic headgear that sets that species apart.

The same is true for a Christian. We can read our Bibles, attend church, and tell everyone that we are followers of Christ. But if we aren't sacrificially loving and serving people in need, we lack the mark. We're simply deer posing as elk.

Prayer

Lord, help me not be a Christian in name only. Help me to have the heart of Christ that loves my neighbors and looks for opportunities to meet their needs. May your Spirit inspire me to be creative, thinking of new ways to solve problems, fix needs, and help in practical ways. Amen.

49

Unimaginably Creative

Scripture Passage: *"And he has filled him with the Spirit of God, with skill, with intelligence, with knowledge, and with all craftsmanship, to devise artistic designs, to work in gold and silver and bronze, in cutting stones for setting, and in carving wood, for work in every skilled craft."* —Exodus 35:31–33

READ: EXODUS 31:1–5

God is unimaginably creative. Just look at the swim bladder of the blowfish, or the plumage of the wood duck, or even the rings around Saturn—these features in creation, and countless more, point to the wildly imaginative nature of God. God made us to share in this attribute when he made us in his image. The first command God gave to Adam and Eve—"be fruitful and multiply"—is a command to create. To form a family is to design and build something meaningful—it's to have children, express values and virtues, and help build a knowledge of and devotion to God within their hearts. Family building is creating.

The Bible is full of stories of faithful people who created things for the glory of God. Noah created an ark from gopher wood. David composed numerous songs and poems. Solomon constructed a temple that held virtually every form of art known to humanity. Musician and author Michael Card writes, "The tabernacle contained every type of representational art: painting, woodworking, sculpting, weaving, metallurgy, ceramics, and more. Throughout every epoch of the Bible, as people sought to be faithful to God and bring honor to his name, they created."[1]

1. Michael Card, *Scribbling in the Sand: Christ and Creativity* (Downers Grove, IL: InterVarsity, 2002), 42.

Some of the most creative people I know are sportsmen. Some express their creativity by tying flies. Some paint pictures of their favorite outdoor moments. Others practice taxidermy. One of my hunting companions, Scott, is an artist with an airbrush. He's won almost every award our state taxidermy association presents because he pays close attention to every vein on the nose of a whitetail, every feather on the back of a pheasant, and every scale on the skin of a rattlesnake. Scott is an artist, helping other people capture and treasure their most exciting moments afield.

We don't typically think of being creative as a command from God. But it is, and like all commands, our joy depends upon our obedience. What's unique about the command to be creative is how powerfully it points people to our Creator. God is the ultimate artist, and everything he's made is good and beautiful—including you and me. He's planted his creative nature deep in our hearts, and when we express this aspect of personhood, we're living out who he made us to be. As you farm or grow food plots, be assured that you're doing it for the glory of God. When you take photographs, paint pictures, or shape things out of wood, do it for the reputation of Christ. When you have children, build homes, or craft sermons, let your ingenuity honor the one who made you. In all things, be creative—it's who God made you to be.

Prayer

God, thank you for the breathtaking world that you have created. You delight me every day with the things that you have made. Help me be creative, finding ways to enjoy this aspect of my character that you have given me. Help my art be something that draws people to you and shows them the greatness of my Creator. Amen.

50

HUNT US DOWN

Scripture Passage: *"So then he has mercy on whomever he wills, and he hardens whomever he wills."* —Romans 9:18

READ: ACTS 9:1-18

I've hunted with some exceptional dogs, but none that could rival Tank. Tank was a chocolate Labrador retriever that could smell a pheasant under three feet of snow from a hundred yards. I'll never forget the time he chased a wounded rooster into the next county and back. My friend Brad shot the bird, and it locked its wings and glided down into the field across the road. Tank bounded after it, weaved in and out of cornstalks, and chased the rooster over the hill and out of sight. If the bird ran to the right, Tank darted right. If the bird went left, Tank went left. The bird couldn't outrun or outsmart that wily lab. Watching Tank, you'd think he was inside that bird's head, anticipating its every move. Shortly after the pursuit began, Tank trotted back across the road, a kicking ringneck locked between his jaws.

The poet Francis Thompson used the image of a hunting dog to describe God. In his poem "The Hound of Heaven," he tells the story of a man who tries to evade God to no avail. When God sets his mind to capture a man's heart and change his life, he will do it successfully. There are few examples more clear in Scripture than the transformation of Saul. In Acts 9:1–2, Saul was chasing Christians and trying to kill anyone who might advance the cause of Christ. He was a bloodthirsty zealot, armed with permission from the Jewish Sanhedrin to destroy those who believed in Jesus. Saul, renamed Paul, later reflected on his hatred of Christians: "And I punished them often in all the synagogues and tried to make them blaspheme, and in raging fury against them I persecuted them even to foreign cities" (Acts 26:11). Saul loathed Jesus and seethed with anger toward anyone who didn't share his view.

But the Hound of Heaven was on Saul's trail. Acts 9:3–9 tells the story of Saul's conversion. He was traveling to Damascus when Jesus knocked him onto the dirt road. Jesus spoke to Saul, opened his eyes, and showed him grace and mercy to such a degree that the cruelest enemy of Christianity became the greatest spokesman of this explosive new movement.

The apostle Paul's transformation is simply one story among hundreds of thousands. It reminds us that Jesus is always the one who pursues. Humans always try to flee from him. Our sin makes us feel ashamed, guilty, and afraid of the God who loves us. If God didn't choose to pursue us, overtake us, and capture us, we would have no hope of becoming his people. But as with Paul, he does hunt us down. In Acts 9:15 the Lord calls Paul "a chosen instrument of mine to carry my name before the Gentiles and kings and the children of Israel." God chose Paul, and God has chosen us, if indeed we walk by faith.

Do you know someone who needs to be captured by the Hound of Heaven? Do *you* need to be radically transformed by the great Pursuer of souls? We are powerless to change our own hearts, let alone the hearts of those we love. But the God who chased down Paul and changed his life can change ours, as well. And if we sense that he's on our trail, we'd be wise to stop running. We can't run, hide, duck, or dodge. He's too good. And if, in his goodness, he decides to capture our hearts and give us eternal life through Jesus, his Son, he's going to do it. Praise God, he's going to do it.

Prayer

Father, I want to be completely and radically "caught" by you. As Paul wrote in Romans 6:18, I want to be a "slave to righteousness," and I know that this happens only when you change a man from the inside out. I submit to you, Father. Please change my life into whatever you have planned for me. Amen.

51

DOING OUR BEST

Scripture Passage: *"Because the poor are plundered, because the needy groan, I will now arise,' says the LORD; 'I will place him in the safety for which he longs.'"*—Psalm 12:5

READ: PHILIPPIANS 2:1–11

Once a year, I make six sets of dark brown eyes light up. I live in rural Nebraska, but my parents live in Lincoln, one of the primary places in America where Sudanese refugees relocate when forced to flee their country. Our extended family has "adopted" a mother and her five children. It's not a legal adoption, but when the Ahmed family arrived in Lincoln from Sudan, they needed help figuring out American culture. My parents took them under their wing, helping them get drivers' licenses, find jobs, and open bank accounts. Our two families have become good friends over the past ten years. Each year, I process and package a deer for them. They love venison, and I can see the appreciation in their eyes.

A predominant theme in the Bible is that God cares about the poor and needy. Isaiah 41:17 says, "When the poor and needy seek water, and there is none, and their tongue is parched with thirst, I the LORD will answer them; I the God of Israel will not forsake them." God promises to provide for those in need, but his plans involve *our* generosity. We are his body, and he often supplies us with more than we need so that we can be generous to others. The apostle Paul emphasized this point when he wrote, "For I do not mean that others should be eased and you burdened, but that as a matter of fairness your abundance at the present time should supply their need, so that their abundance may supply your need, that there may be fairness" (2 Cor. 8:13–14).

I haven't known many sportsmen who are poor. Many have freezers stacked with wild game. They seem to always find money when it's time to upgrade a rod and reel or buy shells for duck season. None of this is wrong—in fact, it is something to feel incredibly thankful for. But it does illustrate how most of us have a tremendous opportunity to provide for the poor and needy.

Who are the "thirsty" among us? Who are the "neighbors" we should be helping? When do we decide to get involved? These are vital questions, and a helpful way to answer them is by thinking about Jesus's command to "love your neighbor *as yourself*" (Mark 12:31, emphasis added). If we will look at those in need and imagine what we would benefit from if we were in their shoes, we will figure out ways to be helpful. If a single mom and her two children are eating frozen pizza or ramen noodles every night, then remember how much you love to eat fresh vegetables, healthy venison steaks, and crispy walleye fillets. Loving this struggling family could involve sharing produce from your garden, game from your freezer, or the day's catch with them. Maybe you know an older man who walks to work every day because he can't afford gas. What if you bought him a gas card or offered him a ride? Our neighbors are those around us, and helping them is as simple as figuring out what we would need if we were in their place.

The last time I gave a cooler of venison to the Ahmeds, the oldest child in the family ran up to me, gave me a hug, and said, "We look forward to this cooler every year! Shoot another one this fall, Mr. Zeke." I promised her I'd do my best.

Prayer

Father, help me see how abundantly blessed I am. You have provided for me in countless ways, now help me provide for others in need. Lord, give me creative ideas and a compassionate heart, that I might see the poor among us and know how to serve them. May my good deeds cause others to see and praise you. Amen.

52

The Sportsman's God

Scripture Passage: *"Therefore God gave them up in the lusts of their hearts to impurity, to the dishonoring of their bodies among themselves, because they exchanged the truth about God for a lie and worshiped and served the creature rather than the Creator, who is blessed forever! Amen."* —Romans 1:24–25

READ: Exodus 20:1–3

I'd ventured into the hunting section of our local sporting goods store over the lunch hour. A young man stood behind the counter, eager to talk about the new line of bows hanging on the racks behind him. When I asked him if he hunted, his face lit up. With unbridled enthusiasm in his voice, he replied, "There's nothing I love more than bowhunting!"

His comment raises an important question: Is it possible for hunting or fishing to become a god to us? And if it is possible, how does this happen? To answer these questions, let's look at the moment when God summoned Moses to the top of Mount Sinai. The very first commandment God gave to Moses was, "You shall have no other gods before me" (Exod. 20:3). "No other gods" is a curious phrase. On one hand, we know from the Bible that there aren't any other gods. The same God who commanded people not to have other gods also declared, "I am God, and there is no other" (Isa. 45:22). However, we have a tendency to treat things that are not gods as if they are gods in our hearts. For example, while Moses was meeting with God on Mount Sinai, his countrymen were making a ridiculous, shiny idol. Even as Moses received the law, Aaron gathered all the gold earrings that Israel had taken from Egypt, melted them down, and formed the gold into the image of a calf.

What turned that bovine into a false god? It became an idol when the people began valuing it more than they valued God. They gave that golden calf their best, putting all their wealth and resources into making it. They put all their time into designing and creating it. And then they agreed together as a community, "Let's worship this thing! Let's make this more valuable in our hearts than anything else." And with that, a golden calf became a god.

Most sportsmen I know don't sacrifice chickens. They don't have altars in their houses filled with wood and metal figurines. But according to the Bible, that doesn't necessarily mean they don't have idols in their lives. Whenever we treasure and pursue something, someone, or some activity *more than* we treasure and pursue God, we have an idol.

When God commanded us to have no other gods, he had our good in mind. He was telling us to keep him central and supreme in our hearts because he's worth it—*infinitely* worth it. And when we value him above all things, we walk in life and joy and spiritual health.

Hunting and fishing are rewarding, exhilarating pastimes. These sports call out an innate desire to be challenged by and have a connection with the great outdoors. But when we make them the most important thing in our hearts, they make horrible gods. They simply cannot satisfy us like the one true God.

Prayer

God, help me keep you first in my heart and my affections. If I have treasured any other person, thing, or activity more than I have treasured you, I repent and ask for your forgiveness. Lord, give me a passion for you that far surpasses my zeal for hunting and fishing. Help me enjoy these sports without worshiping them. Amen.

53

THE GREAT ESCAPE

Scripture Passage: *"But as for the cowardly, the faithless, the detestable, as for murderers, the sexually immoral, sorcerers, idolaters, and all liars, their portion will be in the lake that burns with fire and sulfur, which is the second death."* —Revelation 21:8

READ: 2 THESSALONIANS 1:5–12

One of the most challenging truths in Scripture is the doctrine of hell. How tragic to think that people we love may end up there. I was fishing with a friend awhile back, and between casts he said, "You and I have spent a lot of time together, and we've had a lot of fun, but I can't get over the fact that you think that I'm going to hell when I die."

I kept casting, but my mind wasn't on fishing anymore. I swallowed hard and said, "I hate the idea of you going to hell, but I don't get to make up truths to suit my likings. I trust in the God of the Bible, and in his perfect love and justice. If he promises to judge our sins, I believe he's going to do it."

My friend wanted to know where that truth was found in the Bible, so I pulled out my smartphone, found 2 Thessalonians online, and read the passage out loud. In that passage, Paul tells us that Jesus will return to earth with his angels, "in flaming fire, inflicting vengeance on those who do not know God and on those who do not obey the gospel of our Lord Jesus. They will suffer the punishment of eternal destruction, away from the presence of the Lord and from the glory of his might" (2 Thess. 1:8–9).

Many of us have emotional struggles with these ideas, and we have to admit that there are many things this side of eternity we don't understand. But what we can know for sure is that God, who is perfect in all his ways, will be fair and just when he examines our lives. Because of sin, every person who has ever lived deserves the wrath of God. We have offended an infinite being and deserve an infinite penalty.

What's important to remember about 2 Thessalonians 1:5–12 is that it is not meant to *discourage* us—Paul wrote this passage as encouragement to those who have believed in Jesus. The sting of death and hell is what makes the salve of grace feel so wonderful. Paul wrote this passage to remind Christians that, because they have believed in Jesus, God will defend them, protect them, and one day glorify them in heaven. They will, by grace, be spared hell.

Thinking of my friend in hell not only made me sad, it motivated me to speak the truth of God's Word to him clearly and urgently. I don't enjoy conflict or heavy conversations, but helping my friend see the truth that can rescue him from a terrible eternity was far more important than keeping the peace. I wish I could say that conversation while fishing had a storybook ending. Later, as we docked the boat, he said, "I still don't like the idea of hell or agree with it. But I appreciate that you cared about me enough to tell me what you believe." I replied, "I wouldn't be much of a friend if I didn't."

Our time on this earth is not only limited, it's unpredictably short. This fact is the rock in our shoe that should never let us forget eternity is near. For the love of others, we must speak up now.

Prayer

God, I admit that there is much I don't know and understand about heaven and hell. But I do believe you, and you say that both places are real. Please help me be courageous in sharing the gospel with other people, knowing their eternal lives depend on it. And thank you for the grace you have shown me in your Son, Jesus. Amen.

54

THE FAITH OF
A HOOKER

Scripture Passage: *"You see that a person is justified by works and not by faith alone. And in the same way was not also Rahab the prostitute justified by works when she received the messengers and sent them out by another way? For as the body apart from the spirit is dead, so also faith apart from works is dead."* —James 2:24–26

READ: JOSHUA 2

Rahab had a poor start to life but a tremendous finish. When we first encounter her in Joshua 2, she's a prostitute. Men traveling between home and business would pull off the road in Jericho and spend a few hidden moments in Rahab's bed. As they did, the men no doubt spoke of faraway lands and unique people groups. One of the nations Rahab heard about was Israel and their God, Yahweh. She'd heard how God had rescued Israel from slavery in Egypt. She'd heard about God's provision as his people wandered in the desert. She'd heard about God's promise to give his people a land flowing with milk and honey. She had heard the stories, and they caused an ember of faith to grow in her heart.

That ember fanned into full-orbed faith when the spies showed up at her house. Joshua sent two spies to visit Jericho and survey the land and its people. Something about these spies helped Rahab connect the dots and see that their God was the one true God. Rahab couldn't contain her excitement. She told the men of Israel, "I know that the LORD has given you the land, and that the fear of you has fallen upon us, and that all the inhabitants of the land melt away before you" (Josh. 2:9). This was no small statement of faith. Jericho was a fortress in Canaan. It had stood tall and strong for hundreds of years. But Rahab had heard about

God and his promise to Israel, and she had no doubt that God was faithful.

In spite of her sinful past, Rahab's faith in God landed her a spot in the "heroes of faith" section in Hebrews 11. It is also this faith that the apostle James refers to in his statement: "Was not also Rahab the prostitute justified by works when she received the messengers and sent them out by another way?" (James 2:25).

Many of us have made choices that have deeply hurt us and those we love. We've been selfish. We've chased the wrong things, or the right things to the wrong degree. We've loved and treasured the things God gives us more than God himself. We may not be prostitutes, but we've whored after many pursuits and neglected to keep the Lord first in our affections.

I crossed this line early in my adult life with my passion for deer hunting. For a few years, the Lord took a backseat to my drive to shoot a monster buck. If I wasn't hunting, I was thinking about hunting. I'd flip through hunting catalogs over breakfast, watch videos over the lunch hour, and fall asleep at night reading my favorite hunting magazines. I was crossing lines, treasuring small things when a big God was right there to enjoy. With God's help, I eventually realized my heart was out of balance. I turned to the Lord and asked him to reorient it toward himself.

God loves to answer that prayer. If this is you, if you're crossing lines and hurting those around you, then let Rahab's story bring you great hope. If God was willing to give a prostitute from Jericho a new life and an exciting future based on her genuine faith in the promises of God, then he is willing to do the same for you and me. We just need Rahab's faith.

Prayer

Father, forgive me for chasing the wrong things in life. I want to make you my greatest priority and live a life that is full of faith and grace. Thank you for the story of Rahab and the spies. It shows me that you are a God who forgives and restores when we take a step toward you through faith. Amen.

55

THE WALL
IN THE HEAD

Scripture Passage: *"Therefore, if anyone is in Christ, he is a new creation. The old has passed away; behold, the new has come."* —2 Corinthians 5:17

READ: ROMANS 6:15–23

The Berlin Wall came crashing down in 1989, and along with it came the fence dividing East Germany from Czechoslovakia. Left in its place is a nature preserve bustling with songbirds, elk, and lynx. Birds and animals trek back and forth across the old boundary line without a care in the world. Nothing fears the old line—nothing, that is, except for a red deer named Ahornia. When the wall was operational, it separated two populations of red deer living in the forests of Germany and what is now the Czech Republic. These deer learned that guns, electric fence, and prickly wire guarded the man-made barrier. Ahornia was born eighteen years after the fence came down but still instinctively avoids the boundary line at all costs. Using an electronic collar, wildlife biologists have tracked Ahornia; she will wander many miles around the European forest but will not pass over the old threshold.

How does this happen? How does a completely free deer imprison itself within a border that has been gone for eighteen years? Tom Synnatzschke, a German producer of nature films who has worked in that area of Germany, states, "The wall in the head is still there."[1]

When a man becomes a Christian, he becomes a "new creation." This means that his old, sinful nature is gone. The apostle Paul

1. Tom Synnatzschke, quoted in Cecilie Rohwedder, "Deep in the Forest, Bambi Remains the Cold War's Last Prisoner," *Wall Street Journal*, November 4, 2009, http://online.wsj.com/article/SB125729481234926717.html.

says in Romans 8:2, "For the law of the Spirit of life has set you free in Christ Jesus from the law of sin and death." There is no longer a wall that keeps him imprisoned with the companions of sin and death. He is now able to run and roam freely through the pastures of life and peace. If this is the case, why do we so often still choose sin over life? Why do we still give in to temptations and fall back into damaging patterns? Like Ahornia, we still have a wall in our heads, and it's called our "flesh."

According to the Bible, flesh is our tendency to try to meet our longings for acceptance, self-worth, and significance through our own abilities. When we operate in our flesh, we set aside God and we go it alone, relying on ourselves to find joy, peace, and a sense of significance. When we trust in Jesus for our salvation, we still have many habits and tendencies ingrained in our flesh. Like wildlife thoughtlessly walking along a deeply rutted game trail, we can fall back into the habits of looking to self to satisfy our needs. We must daily remind one another that the Spirit of God is present to help us learn to live in our new freedom. We must continually speak the truth to our hearts that we are free from sin and death and can now choose faithfulness, obedience, and joy. And we must pray and ask God's Spirit to do his great work of sanctification in our hearts, teaching us to roam free in our new life in Christ.

Prayer

Father, by your Spirit, free me from my fleshly desires to live for myself. Help me recognize when I'm putting myself ahead of you and striving in my own power to find significance or acceptance. Help me understand and embrace the gospel of grace, that I might walk by your Spirit, free from my old habits and sins. Amen.

56

SEEING MYSELF
IN THE DRUNK

Scripture Passage: *"Go and learn what this means,
'I desire mercy, and not sacrifice.'"* —Matthew 9:13

READ: PSALM 123

My family was lounging on the deck of the cabin after a full day
of fishing. We were staying at a resort on Table Rock Lake in
Missouri, swimming, grilling out, and teaching the kids to angle
for bass. When I travel, I always request the cabin farthest from
the lodge. I like to be situated away from the parking lot, the pool,
and the hub of activity.

Earlier, when we were docking the boat, a group of about twenty
college students carried boxes of beer into the lodge for a night of
partying. Two hours later, as my kids caught fireflies in the courtyard
in front of our room, three highly intoxicated young men stumbled
toward our cabin. They were smoking, swearing, and numerically
ranking the women they'd left behind in the lodge. As they got
closer and louder, I was becoming more and more attentive. I also
sensed that I was growing more and more self-righteous. I started
having thoughts like, "I'm glad I'm not like these guys" and "Why
don't they pull it together, grow up, and stop being such jerks?"
By the time they had walked past our cabin, I'd had a dozen such
thoughts go through my mind.

In that moment, my son ran up to me and said, "Dad, I don't
think those guys know Jesus. We should pray for them." My son
sounded like such an adult; I felt like such a child. His comment
reminded me of what Jesus said when some uppity, self-righteous
Pharisees criticized him for eating with tax collectors: "I desire
mercy, and not sacrifice" (Matt. 9:13). His point is, "I want my
followers to share my heart for sinners, not think that being a

Christian is going through rituals, performing good deeds, or being better than others."

A person who understands what God has done for him by grace will look into the faces of drunkards, liars, cheaters, adulterers, murderers, prisoners, prostitutes, and druggies, and he will see himself. If I had been thinking about God's grace, I would have seen those men walking by as a chance to look in the mirror. I once was a man like them. And I still would be but for the grace of God.

God wants us, who have received such amazing mercy, to carry a heart of love for those who have yet to meet our merciful God. I replied to my son, "You're right, buddy. Let's pray for them tonight before bed." Immediately after I said that, the three guys walked up to our cabin and started talking with us. I introduced my family to them, and we had a good talk before they stumbled off into the dark. I spoke with kindness and compassion, without the judgmental attitude I had been carrying just a few moments prior. All because my ten-year-old son reminded me to see myself in the drunk.

Prayer

Jesus, help me see myself in the sinner, always remembering the grace you have shown me. Help me to be motivated by your generosity and love, and help me not neglect those around me who are still stuck in sin and rebellion. By your Spirit, help me not miss an opportunity to share the gospel with those who need to hear it. Amen.

57

Fetch It Up

Scripture Passage: *"Let us draw near with a true heart in full assurance of faith, with our hearts sprinkled clean from an evil conscience and our bodies washed with pure water."* —Hebrews 10:22

Read: Luke 15:11–32

A shamed dog won't fetch. One day when he was a puppy, I spent an hour training my German wirehair, Ezra. I'd throw his canvas bumper and he'd sit by my side, wagging his tail and waiting for me to give the command "Fetch it up!" When I said those words, he'd retrieve the bumper and place it in my hand. We must have repeated the game thirty times that afternoon; it was pure pleasure for both of us.

The next day Ezra snuck into the chicken coop and wounded one of our Rhode Island Red hens. I summoned my deepest, most authoritative tone of voice and let Ezra have it. I yelled at him for the better part of ten minutes. Later that afternoon, when I grabbed Ezra's bumper and tried to initiate another game of fetch, he just wouldn't do it. He lay by my side and looked up at me with droopy, guilt-ridden eyes.

Many Christians go through life like my shamed dog. We feel guilty and dirty around God, so we cower in the corner, trying not to make eye contact with him and hoping that he'll put up with us. God wants something more for us. Most people are familiar with the parable of the prodigal son from Luke 15. When this young Jewish boy asked for his father's money and then squandered it into Gentile hands, he shamed his father and his family. Jewish culture employed what was called a *kezazah* ceremony for such a shameful act. If a young man tried to return home after losing his Jewish family's money to Gentiles, the townsfolk would meet him at the city limits and break a large pot in front of the boy, symbolically displaying that the town viewed him as a shameful disgrace. This ceremony would sever all ties between the boy and his community.[1]

Jesus's listeners would have known of this ceremony and would have assumed this to be an appropriate fate for the boy trying to return home. But something spectacular happens in the story. The father watches for his son. Upon seeing him approach the village, he hitches up his garments and races down the dusty city street to welcome the boy home and cut off any attempts to exercise the *kezazah* ceremony. If the man was a well-respected farmer in that village, it would have been terribly inappropriate and undignified for him to expose his legs and run through the city streets. It would also have been viewed as shameful for this father to welcome and restore his son. It wasn't what the boy deserved. But it is what this father, who represents God, chose to do in order to restore his son.[2]

This story is a reminder to us that when Jesus faced the cross and the crowds of people who mocked, shamed, and despised him, he bore our shame. Because of our sins, we are guilty, and if we got what we deserved, we would be right to feel ashamed and guilty. But we didn't get what we deserve. Jesus took our punishment. We no longer live at the feet of God, looking up at him with eyes of regret. We now walk with him as his sons, knowing that at all times we are fully pleasing and acceptable to him because of Jesus. Do you believe this? If so, live a shame-free life—you are a son of God now.

Prayer

Father, thank you for loving me so much that while I was still a sinner, you sent your Son to win me back. I cannot express my gratitude for your amazing grace. Help me know that I am pleasing to you at all times, and may that new identity motivate me to live a life worthy of your sacrifice. Amen.

1. Kenneth Bailey, *Jacob & the Prodigal: How Jesus Retold Israel's Story* (Downers Grove, IL: InterVarsity, 2003), 102.
2. Ibid., 108–9.

58

KNOWING YOU
ARE KNOWN

Scripture Passage: *"I am the good shepherd. I know my own and my own know me, just as the Father knows me and I know the Father; and I lay down my life for the sheep."* —John 10:14–15

READ: PSALM 139:1–16

I got to know a bird one afternoon along the Niobrara River in northern Nebraska. I'd positioned my ground blind at the top of a hill amidst a crowd of dying cottonwoods. I had watched four toms fan out and strut on this site the afternoon before. After situating myself in the blind, I looked through the window and saw a bright blue speck flittering through the air toward my tent. The bird landed a few yards away, then hopped around looking for something to eat for about an hour. I had my smartphone, so I did a little research on my feathery friend while he feasted on grubs. I discovered that the bird was an Indigo Bunting, which ranges from Canada to Florida, using the stars at night to direct its migration.

That was about five years ago, and since then I recognize and enjoy Indigo Buntings every time I see them. These birds feel familiar to me now. This is what happens when we learn the name of something or someone. Two people can take the same walk in the wilderness; one can see a large tree with knobby bark, while the other sees a fifty-year-old hackberry. One may notice a large furry creature dart across the path, while the other recognizes a woodchuck. One sees a deer bounding through the woods, while the other recognizes that it's a 3½-year-old whitetail with palmated antlers. To name something is to know something, and to know something is to be familiar with it. Many of my favorite sportsmen and conservationists—such as Wendell Berry, John Muir, and Aldo Leopold—journaled. These men paid attention to their environment, recorded their time afield, and made it a point to name and acquaint themselves with the animals and trees around them.

In Psalm 139, we see that the God who created us is intimately familiar with us. He knows when we sit down and when we rise up. He knows our thoughts, paths, and ways. He knows every cell in our body because, as David writes, "[God's] eyes saw my unformed substance; in your book were written, every one of them, the days that were formed for me, when as yet there was none of them" (Ps. 139:16). Before he created us, God knew our name and had designs for our lives.

Deism is the belief that God created the natural processes of the earth, then stepped away from any personal interaction with his creation. But this isn't the God of the Bible. The Scriptures tell us that God cares deeply about his creation because he designed it, named it, and relates with it. If you ever question whether God knows you and cares about even the smallest aspect of your life, just remember how deeply you care about the things you have named.

Prayer

God, thank you for your love toward me. I'm so glad that my life wasn't accidental or random, but rather it was planned by you from the foundations of time. Help me trust your care for me. Amen.

59

HAPPENSTANCE

Scripture Passage: *"Whatever the LORD pleases, he does, in heaven and on earth, in the seas and all deeps."* —Psalm 135:6

READ: JOB 38–39

I've seen some wonderful, awe-inspiring things in the woods. I've watched a doe stand on her back legs in order to nibble the tip of a small elm tree. I've seen two young bucks fight like street brawlers. And I've witnessed a doe bathe her fawn, licking every inch and every spot, before the two lay down together for a midmorning nap. John Muir said, "In every walk with nature one receives far more than he seeks." This is what sportsmen love about spending time outside—we never know what we will see.

It can all seem so random, so left to chance. One deer turns left, walks fifty paces, and presents a shot. Another goes right, stops, and hides behind a tree. Some will run into the sides of semitrucks traveling the highways.

The Bible describes a God who not only created all things but is also still engaged in his creation. He directs the snow and the rain (Job 37:6), freezes the lakes and ponds in winter (37:10), and even causes hawks to soar and spread their wings (39:26). He has shut the mouths of lions (Dan. 6:22), commanded ravens to bring a prophet food (1 Kings 17:4), and determines migration times of the stork, turtledove, swallow, and crane (Jer. 8:7).

"Ask the animals, and they will teach you. Ask the birds of the sky, and they will tell you. Speak to the earth, and it will instruct you. Let the fish in the sea speak to you. For they all know that my disaster has come from the hand of the LORD. For the life of every living thing is in his hand, and the breath of every human being" (Job 12:7–10 NLT).

IN PURSUIT

The wonder of the woods isn't random. It's brimming with purpose. We rarely understand the specific reasons why God does what he does, but that's okay. Our hope and happiness isn't tied to knowing why. It's tied to knowing *who*. If we know who is in control, then we know that life isn't meaningless. We also know that we can trust God with every event in creation.

As hunters and fishermen, we'll spend over a hundred million hours outside this fall. When we go outdoors, nature takes us by the hand and leads us into deep ponderings, thoughts, and questions. A tree causes us to consider time and age. A flock of geese flying south stimulates thoughts about the seasons of life. A wild and winding river causes us to contemplate the simultaneous smallness and greatness of our lives. May all of it cause us to thank our Creator. As William Shakespeare wrote, "This our life, exempt from public haunt, finds tongues in trees, books in the running brooks, sermons in stones, and good in every thing."[1]

Prayer

Father, thank you for this earth you created. Help me appreciate you every time I see your creation. Help me know that you sovereignly and mysteriously govern all the things you have made. Give me a deep trust in you and a knowledge that nothing in life is random. Amen.

1. *As You Like It*, act 2, scene 1, lines 15–17.

60

LEPROSY OF
THE HEART

Scripture Passage: *"Because, if you confess with your mouth that Jesus is Lord and believe in your heart that God raised him from the dead, you will be saved."*
—Romans 10:9

READ: 2 KINGS 5:1–14

Powerful people have a hard time with simple solutions. I shared a tent with a wealthy businessman during an eight-day moose hunt a few years back. One night, after a grueling day of walking up and down mountains, we rested on our cots and talked about our lives. When I asked him about his wife, he stated, "Zeke, I'll give you $10,000 if you will fix my marriage." I suggested to him that he start by taking his wife out on dates, asking her questions about her life, and showing tenderness through his words and actions. The light of the lantern hanging inside the tent revealed a confused expression. He replied, "Nah . . . I don't think that would work. That sounds too simplistic."

Naaman, the commander of the Syrian army, was an important person who had a hard time with a simple solution. He had leprosy, a bacteria that produces lumps, sores, and lesions on the skin. Leprosy typically causes people to lose sensation in their nerves, which leads to inadvertent self-injury. Naaman had this tragic disease, and his servant girl from Israel had the solution. The young woman suggested that Naaman visit the prophet Elisha in her home country. She knew Elisha was a man of God who could help Naaman.

So Naaman packed up his bags and headed to Israel. But instead of going straight to Elisha, he went to the king. "Important people should go to important people for help," Naaman thought. But the king couldn't help Naaman, because the king had even less faith in God than this leprous man from Syria. When Naaman asked the king of Israel for healing, the king panicked, thinking Naaman was tricking him into battle.

Elisha heard of Naaman's request and sent word to the king to send Naaman to him. Naaman reluctantly went, but when he arrived at Elisha's house, Elisha didn't even come out to greet this powerful man. Instead, he sent a messenger to tell the commander to wash in the Jordan River seven times. Naaman was furious. Not only had the king turned him away, but this unimportant Israelite prophet wouldn't even speak to him. And now he was to bathe in a filthy little river in Israel? "Doesn't he know who he's dealing with? If he did, he'd come up with a bigger and better solution," Naaman assumed. But as he left Elisha's house in rage, a servant convinced him to try Elisha's advice. After Naaman's seventh submersion in the river, "his flesh was restored like the flesh of a little child, and he was clean" (2 Kings 5:14).

This Old Testament story teaches us a vital truth about life with God: our deepest problems aren't happening on the outside of our bodies. The sickness of sin and self-reliance is what ruins our lives. Naaman was a proud man, and his pride almost kept him from experiencing the saving power of God. We too have pride, and it can keep us from trusting in Jesus as our Lord and Savior. Naaman needed just enough faith to obey the Word of the Lord and wash in the river seven times. Likewise, we need to humble ourselves and trust in Jesus's death and resurrection in order to be saved from our leprosy of heart.

A sincere trust in God's grace holds the power to change everything in life. Don't let the simplicity of God's rescue plan keep you from his willingness to transform yours.

Prayer

Holy Spirit, please melt my heart of stone. I depend on myself for so many things, but I cannot fix the problem of sin or heal the sickness of my heart. Give me the faith to trust in the life and death of Jesus for the forgiveness of my sins. Give me a heart that is whole and healthy that I may walk in your ways, Lord. Amen.

61

PLAYFUL CHRISTIANITY

Scripture Passage: *"How beautiful upon the mountains are the feet of him who brings good news, who publishes peace, who brings good news of happiness, who publishes salvation, who says to Zion, 'Your God reigns.'"*—Isaiah 52:7

READ: ROMANS 10:13-17

Herman Melville, the author of the great man-versus-beast story, *Moby Dick*, also wrote *White-Jacket*, a novel loosely based on his experiences as a seaman aboard the frigate USS *United States*. Melville tells a story of gross neglect involving the ship's surgeon, Cadwallader Cuticle, MD. A sailor tries to escape the ship and is shot in the leg by an officer on deck. The sailor is rushed to Dr. Cuticle, who is so excited about the incident that he invites doctors and surgeons from other vessels to come aboard and watch the leg surgery. With his audience gathered, he begins to lecture on anatomy, surgical techniques, and even his own impressive resume. Meanwhile, the bleeding sailor moans and wails and begs for help. Undeterred, Dr. Cuticle continues to lecture, stressing the severity of the sailor's injury.

As he drones on, the ship's steward interrupts and respectfully reports, "Please, sir, the patient is dead."

Unaffected, the good doctor professionally replies, "I predicted that the operation might prove fatal; he was very much run down."[1]

Our culture seems to share Dr. Cuticle's complacency about death. Many of our country's forefathers feared God and viewed life with a sense of sobriety. They understood that the days were short and evil, and all people must choose heaven or hell, life or death, salvation through faith alone in Jesus or an eternal life separated

1. Herman Melville, *White-Jacket*, Library of America series (New York: Viking, 1983), 617ff.

from God. Congregations met with a sense of urgency. Sermons were preached with a wartime mentality. Hymns were written that emphasized the battle for souls taking place all around. In 1865, Sabine Baring-Gould wrote the song "Onward, Christian Soldiers," to be sung by children and adults in a marching formation. The hymn celebrates how Jesus leads us into battle against the great enemy of man. Christians were urged to carry a warfare mentality that urged them to diligence and faithfulness.

The Scriptures haven't changed. The urgency of life, death, and eternity hasn't lessened. And souls are no less important in the twenty-first century than they were in the nineteenth. But the attitude of many Christians is radically different. A. W. Tozer writes, "Men think of the world, not as a battleground, but as a playground. We are not here to fight, we are here to frolic."[2]

As strong men of faith, we must not lead our families, friends, and spiritual communities into a playful sort of Christian life. There are times to hunt, fish, and have fun with others, but walking faithfully with Jesus means rightly understanding that we are always in a battle against a real enemy, and the eternal destinies of many people are at stake. May we, even in our times of rest and recreation, be on our guard. And may we share the truths of Christ with others who are under attack.

Prayer

Jesus, help me appreciate that every moment of every day is important. Teach me, Lord, to number my days so I may gain a heart of wisdom. Help me believe in heaven and hell, and feel urgency deep in my bones. Amen.

2. A. W. Tozer, "This World: Playground or Battleground," in *The Best of A. W. Tozer: 52 Favorite Chapters*, comp. Warren W. Wiersbe (Grand Rapids: Baker, 1978), 85.

62

A REFUSAL OF LIES

Scripture Passage: *"Sanctify them in the truth; your word is truth."* —John 17:17

READ: 1 PETER 5:6–11

One of the best ways to fool a trout into taking your fly is to "match the hatch." I fly-fished the South Platte River this summer, and as I entered the water, a bug landed on my neck. I reached back, grabbed the insect, and placed it on the ground by my fly boxes. It was a pale morning dun with a brown body and translucent wings. I found a fly in my box that closely matched the insect, then tied it onto the end of my tippet. On the third cast, a fifteen-inch rainbow snatched the fly, giving me a thrilling five-minute fight.

The more effectively you deceive a fish with something close to the real thing, the more fish you'll catch. The enemy of our souls works in a similar way. Instead of matching the hatch and deceiving us with insects, he matches a lie with a corresponding truth from God's Word and deceives us into believing something false. For example, when God tells us we were made to enjoy sex in a loving, committed marriage relationship, Satan presents the lie that we can find happiness in any sexual experience we want, inside or outside of marriage. Another example comes to mind: God made us to work and find a sense of enjoyment in being creative and productive. Satan comes after us with the lie that our work holds enough power to make us feel fully significant and important, and we can find true fulfillment if we throw ourselves into it headlong. Satan doesn't need to be all that creative; he just needs to mimic a truth closely enough to fool us into biting.

How do we snatch the truth of God and avoid the lies of our enemy? By becoming so familiar with God's Word that Satan's lies are easily spotted. Every now and then a fly fisherman encounters a wise old trout that has figured out the game. He can spot a fake fly floating on the surface, and rather than taking the hook into his mouth, he does what's called a "refusal"—the trout rises, grabs the fly with the tip of his mouth, and decides it's fake. He quickly spits the fly out and swims away. You try your best to set the hook, but there's nothing there.

We must learn to spot and refuse the lies of our enemy. Do you know a man who lives a wise, thoughtful life? He likely has learned to examine a thought, feeling, or idea, recognize when it's true and when it's false, and then leave the counterfeit options behind. This wisdom and discernment is available to each of us. We simply need to become so familiar with the truth that the lies are easily exposed.

Prayer

God, help me know your Word accurately so I can recognize a lie from my enemy and choose not to believe it. Give me the discipline of mind and heart to read, study, and memorize your Word. Plant your truths deep in my heart, Father. Amen.

63

JAWING WITH GOD

Scripture Passage: *"And when you pray, do not heap up empty phrases as the Gentiles do, for they think that they will be heard for their many words."* —Matthew 6:7

READ: MATTHEW 6:5–15

The longer I walk with God, the less fancy my words become. I remember the first sermon I delivered after graduating from seminary. I preached about God's love, and I inserted a handful of hundred-dollar, ivory tower words into my message. Then, I loaded my prayer with more lofty terms I'd picked up in my studies. This is what the Jewish Pharisees did when they spoke and prayed. The Pharisees were the religious leaders in Jerusalem, and they would pray long, weighty prayers out loud in the middle of the street, so everyone could hear them. They wanted crowds to watch. They wanted people to be impressed. They wanted others to think they were extra holy. Looking back on my early days in ministry, I'm embarrassed to admit that some of those same motives were present in my heart.

When Jesus left the infinite glories of heaven to be born in a dingy stable among dirty animals, he removed all religious pretense. What's more, when Jesus grew up and began his ministry, he called common fishermen to be his disciples, ate dinner in a corrupt tax collector's home, and spent time talking with an outcast Samaritan woman. Jesus showed that God is not impressed with high and lofty speech from uppity, prideful people. When we talk with God, we must speak authentically, from the heart, about the things that matter most to us.

Jesus knew that people would always have questions about prayer, so he offered a basic but profound example for us to follow: Ask God to make his name holy, or special, in your heart. Ask him to continue breaking into this world with his truth and his purposes. Ask him to continue to provide for you, forgive your sins, and give you a heart that desires to forgive others. And ask him to help you avoid temptation and sin's tug on your heart. These are the basics—Prayer 101—and we must never move beyond these vital truths.

I took my ten-year-old son, Aidan, hunting the other day. I typically say a short prayer before I go afield, but on this day, as we were driving out of the driveway, Aidan asked if he could pray. From the backseat, he said these words: "God, thanks for this time with my dad. Thanks for making trees and deer. Please keep us safe. And help daddy to make a good shot if we see a big buck. Amen."

My son's prayer was straight shooting, right from his heart. He wasn't trying to sound showy or extra spiritual. He wasn't trying to impress me. He was simply talking with the God who would be with us on the outing. This is how God wants us all to jaw with him. He is our Father, and he knows what we need before we ask him for it. As our Father, his heart is for us. He can't wait to give us what we need. He knows what will delight our hearts. Psalm 37:4 reminds us, "Delight yourself in the LORD, and he will give you the desires of your heart."

On this day, when you speak with God, be yourself. Talk as if you're with a family member or your closest friend. Don't worry about cadence or polish. Don't worry about using fancy, theological words. Just talk about the things that matter most to you, as if you are with your closest companion—because you are.

Prayer

Father, help me be comfortable in my own skin, just as you have made me. Help me not worry about impressing other people, or you, with the words that I say. I want to be a man who speaks plainly the things that are on my heart. For your glory, I ask. Amen.

64

PALPABLE PRESENCE

Scripture Passage: *"Train up a child in the way he should go; even when he is old he will not depart from it."* —Proverbs 22:6

READ: EPHESIANS 6:1–4

I spent a day walking fields for pheasant with Don, a fifty-year-old man from eastern Nebraska. We had a successful hunt, and our team of six had our limit by lunch. As we filled up on fried chicken and mashed potatoes at the local diner, Don said, "Today was bittersweet for me. My dad taught me to hunt, and we spent hours together walking those same fields we just hunted." He paused, then added, "I felt like he was walking beside me all morning."

I love how Nathan Miller describes Teddy Roosevelt's father in his book *Theodore Roosevelt: A Life*: "No one had a greater influence upon his namesake. By example and instruction, he imbued Theodore, Jr., with a strong sense of moral values and remained an almost palpable presence at his side long after his death at the age of forty-six."[1]

There's no shortcut to becoming a good father. It takes showing sincere interest in our children's lives. It involves tucking them in at night, praying with them at mealtimes, and sharing our difficulties and successes with them. It means taking our daughters on dates, or taking our sons on adventures. To be a good father, we need to wrestle, read, fish, tickle, shop, camp, and play games with our children. Fatherhood requires time.

Biblically, a father's two main roles in his children's lives are to train and discipline. Both words are pregnant with meaning. To train a child means to initiate and model life according to God's

1. Nathan Miller, *Theodore Roosevelt: A Life* (New York: HarperCollins, 2003), 32.

commands and statutes. It implies that a father will know God's Word and take the lead role in educating his children in it—but in a do-as-I-do sort of way, not in a preachy, heavy-handed, do-as-I-say manner.

To discipline means to instruct, warn, and chastise. It involves setting clear boundaries and rules based on truth and love. When children break those boundaries and rules, a faithful father lovingly corrects, teaches, guides, and provides consequences for them. The goal of discipline is to help our children learn that wrong, sinful choices have painful consequences. We want them to grow in their Christlikeness, learning to think, feel, and act like Jesus.

These two biblical ideas together cast a vision for fathers to model life for their children, spending great amounts of time together and showing their sons and daughters what it looks like to walk with God at home, at work, and in the public square. Proverbs 22:6 teaches us that if we take our role as fathers seriously, training and disciplining our children every day, we have done our part to help them learn to walk with the Lord themselves.

Our children's decisions of whether or not to walk with God are out of our hands. However, if we fathers choose to be faithful to God and intentional in our interactions with our children, we will give them a vision for living with God. That's a powerful gift to give our children.

Fathers, let's not fill up our schedules to the point that we don't have time to spend training, encouraging, and discipling our children. We may one day regret the amount of time we spent at the office or outside chasing our pursuits, but we will never regret the time we spent building into our children's lives. And neither will they.

Prayer

Father, I want to be a father in the manner that you are a Father. I want to be kind, loving, patient, and fully engaged in my children's lives. By your Spirit, help me be a good dad every day. I want to be a palpable presence for good in my children's lives, long after I meet you face-to-face. Amen.

65

A FORCE FOR
GOOD

Scripture Passage: *"As for you, brothers, do not grow weary in doing good."* —2 Thessalonians 3:13

READ: JEREMIAH 29:1-14

The film *127 Hours* tells the story of a twenty-seven-year-old man, Aron Ralston, who wants to be alone. The movie opens with Aron racing to the wilderness, dismissing phone calls from his mom and sister, and ignoring an inquiry from his boss on where he's going. He's got his headphones on and doesn't want anyone else in his world. Then Aron gets in trouble; he falls into a deep canyon in the mountains of southeastern Utah, and his right arm ends up lodged between a chockstone and the wall of a crevice. After surviving for five days on 500 ml of water, Aron uses a dull knife to saw through flesh, muscle, and nerves in order to amputate his arm and free himself.

As Aron is struggling for his life, he keeps coming back to a memory of his old girlfriend telling him, "You're going to be so lonely, Aron." Her statements haunt him and help him recognize that the choice to be self-centered and isolated from others is leading him down a dangerous path. During his fight to survive, he imagines the life he wants to have: married, with children, living in community with others.

There's something alluring about the idea of rugged individualism. We often think we'll be happier and more content if we go it alone. People are complicated and relationships can be so messy and time-consuming, so we enter a self-imposed exile from the people around us. But there is no life and joy in isolation.

When Israel was taken captive by Babylon in 586 BC, God told his people how to make the most of their lives:

Build houses and live in them; plant gardens and eat their produce. Take wives and have sons and daughters; take wives for your sons, and give your daughters in marriage, that they may bear sons and daughters; multiply there, and do not decrease. But seek the welfare of the city where I have sent you into exile, and pray to the LORD on its behalf, for in its welfare you will find your welfare. (Jer. 29:5–7)

What a powerful idea: our welfare is intimately connected to the welfare of our local community. This is a countercultural way of living. We so often think we need to distance ourselves from or outcompete our neighbors in order to "get ahead." This is how the Israelites felt about the Babylonians, the enemy that had destroyed their temple and forced them to relocate. But God told his people that the best thing they could do for themselves was serve their community.

How can we, God's people, benefit our communities? By planting gardens, strengthening relational roots, praying together, and working toward the success of our neighbors. Brothers, may we be the most active, helpful, contributing members of our local community. When everyone wins, we win.

Prayer

Lord, help me be known in my town as a positive force for good. Help me contribute to those in need. Help me plant my roots deep into the place you have me, trusting that my welfare is in my commitment to my local community. May you look great through the testimony of my life. Amen.

66

The Horn of Humility

Scripture Passage: *"But this is the one to whom I will look: he who is humble and contrite in spirit and trembles at my word."* —Isaiah 66:2

READ: ISAIAH 66:1-2

In J. R. R. Tolkien's *The Lord of the Rings*, Boromir carries the Horn of Gondor, a large war horn "of the wild ox of the East, bound with silver, and written in ancient characters."[1] For countless generations past, the oldest son of the house of the Stewards of Gondor had wielded the horn, using it to summon help during battle. Legend surrounding the horn said, "If it be blown at need anywhere within the bounds of Gondor, as the realm was of old, its voice will not pass unheeded."[2] Blowing the horn meant help was on the way.

Pride is one of our worst enemies. Our self-sufficiency and sense of ego lead us into dark, lonely places. Our pride can cause us to get tangled up in the throes of an addiction and not ask for help. It can encourage us to bend rules to the point that we no longer care about what's right and what's wrong. It can lead to a lifestyle of lies and deceit.

I know a man, Greg, who has been actively involved with pornography for the past thirty years. To avoid convicting internet evidence, he used movies and videos to feed his addiction. Things progressed to such a sad place that he'd sneak out of bed in the middle of the night, drive to a convenience store and rent a pornographic movie, then return the movie and get back into bed before his wife's alarm would go off in the morning. His heart was sick and dying, yet his pride kept him from crying out for help.

1. J. R. R. Tolkien, *The Two Towers* (New York: Del Rey, 2012), 307.
2. Ibid.

Our pride doesn't need to do us in. There is a way for us to blow a horn and cry for help. The Bible calls it *humility*. Like the Horn of Gondor, a man who humbles himself and cries out to God will always be heard and helped. God is omniscient, meaning that he knows all things. And he is omnipresent, which means that he is always present in all places. Yet, Isaiah 66:2 states that God, in a personal manner, at times turns his attention to a particular person: "he who is humble and contrite in spirit and trembles at my word."

God rescues sinful men who choose to cry out to him for help. The last time Boromir blew the Horn of Gondor, his friends arrived too late. Enemies had killed Boromir and kidnapped his hobbit companions. Boromir's rescuers failed to get there in time. But God will never fail to help nor be tardy in meeting the needs of those who cry out to him in humility. If you are stuck in a sin or a cycle of pride and ego, the help of God is as near to you as the willingness to submit to him from a broken, contrite heart. All you need to do is confess your sins and receive God's grace.

My friend Greg, after decades of struggling with porn, humbled himself and cried out to God to rescue him. God showed up and provided a path out of that addiction. Greg and his wife went through treatment and joined a support group at their church. Greg blew the horn of humility, and God arrived in time. And God will do this for you, as well, if you will blow the horn of humility.

Prayer

Jesus, help me be humble enough to call out to you when I am battling with my pride and ego. Break my back if I won't bow to you. I know that my joy is in walking humbly with you, keeping you as the central and supreme person in my life . . . not myself. Amen.

67

THE VAPOROUS LIFE

Scripture Passage: *"Yet you do not know what to-morrow will bring. What is your life? For you are a mist that appears for a little time and then vanishes."*
—James 4:14

READ: JOB 14

Life is fleeting. I was reminded of this awhile back as I helped a family through a horrible tragedy. Jessica and her husband, Rick, were setting out for home after a night of good conversation with friends. It was frigid outside, and the wind blew waves of snow over the dormant cornfields lining the gravel road. Their heater was still warming up as they turned onto the highway. A mile down the road, an oncoming truck struck a whitetail deer and sent it flying through the air. The doe, as if thrown intentionally, came crashing through Jessica's side of the windshield. One leg punctured the backseat and came to rest on the spare tire. Seventeen minutes after hugging their friends and saying good night, a rescue team found Rick, still holding his wife's hand, now numb from the stillness of death.

James 4:14 tells us that our lives "are a mist that appears for a little time and then vanishes." This statement is intended to humble us, reminding us that we are not the masters of our destiny. We make our plans, expecting all our dreams to come true. Yet not one of us knows what tomorrow holds. Mike Mason says, "Lives are curliques of fire cut briefly in the dark with a glowing stick."[1]

The man who makes the most of his life is the man who lives with an eye toward his death. What do you want to be true about you at your funeral? Do you want to die with all your

1. Mike Mason, *The Mystery of Marriage: Meditations on the Miracle* (Portland, OR: Multnomah, 1985), 71.

relationships intact? Put them in order today, asking forgiveness from those you've hurt and granting forgiveness to those who have offended you.

Do you want to have people say about you, "He loved God more than anything in life"? Then be someone who deeply desires God today, and pursue him through obedience, prayer, and spending time with his people.

Do you want to have treasure in heaven? Then invest your heart, possessions, and time into the things of eternity . . . right now. Keeping an eye on the end has a powerful way of impacting how we live today.

A few months after Jessica's death, I had lunch with her brother, Tim. I asked Tim how Rick was holding up, and he replied, "He's still in tremendous pain . . . always will be, I'm sure. But he looks at life differently now. He doesn't take a single moment for granted anymore."

As I drove away from the restaurant, I prayed for Rick and thanked God for the wisdom he had given this man. Then I prayed for myself and asked God for that same wisdom—the moment-by-moment realization that we are living a vaporous life. For it is in the reflection of our death that we will truly live.

Prayer

Father, don't let me go through life as an ignorant person who never thinks of my own death. Help me to number my days and make the most of every moment you give me. Help me reach the moments before my death with no large, glaring regrets. I need your help to live this way, Father. Amen.

68

NO SHORTCUTS

Scripture Passage: *"But seek first the kingdom of God and his righteousness, and all these things will be added to you."* —Matthew 6:33

READ: ISAIAH 55:6–7

President Jimmy Carter is a sportsman. He grew up reading Zane Grey, Jack London, and John Muir. He developed a passion for hunting quail and angling for trout at an early age, and Georgia was the perfect state for him to pursue these interests. In his later years, he's teaching his children and grandchildren how to fish and enjoy the great outdoors. As a sportsman, President Carter understands the sacrifice involved in pursuing game. He writes, "It is almost inherent in the seeking of wild things in their native habitat that you must forgo many of the comfortable trappings of civilization."[1] All true and successful sportsmen understand what Carter means—to find success afield or on the water, we must have a sharp focus and be willing to sacrifice comfort and convenience in order to outsmart our prey.

One of the most challenging passages in the Bible is Matthew 6:33, especially Jesus's statement, "Seek first the kingdom of God." This command challenges us at the core of our affections, because we tend to seek first our own wants and needs. We want to feel comfortable. We want to live in peace with our friends and families. We want financial security, physical health, and happiness. These are natural desires, but Jesus's command informs us that those interests are no longer primary. If we follow Jesus, we must desire the kingdom of God and the glory of the King above all other interests and pursuits. We must have a sharp focus and

1. Jimmy Carter, "A Childhood Outdoors," *A Hunter's Heart: Honest Essays on Blood Sport*, collected by David Petersen (New York: Owl Books, 1996), 44.

be willing to sacrifice comfort and convenience in order to keep the kingdom our priority.

If something is worth acquiring, it's worth the sacrifice required. I recently returned from a fishing trip to Colorado. I planned that trip two months in advance, tested my gear, read about the region, and purchased the flies other anglers suggested. On the day I fished Cheesman Canyon, I woke up early, packed a lunch and my gear, and then made the half-mile trek up the mountain (in waders) and into the river valley. I fished for eight hours straight, tying on a new fly every fifteen minutes. What did all that sacrifice and effort bring me? I caught a seventeen-inch, bright, energetic rainbow trout that fought my line for about three minutes before I could net it. The effort and sacrifice was well worth the thrill of that moment.

To seek first God's kingdom is similar to all the work and planning that goes into a fishing or hunting trip, but it's even more demanding. Pursuing God above all things is a lifelong adventure, not something that culminates in a moment of time. It requires activities that men often try to avoid—reading, praying, and attending church. To do the work, a man must believe in his heart that the pleasures of knowing God intimately are worth the sacrifices required to experience him. It's one thing to trust in Christ and know that you are saved, it's another thing altogether to go through your days knowing God's presence is with you, encouraging you and giving you everything you need for each moment. To experience that closeness to God, we must seek him above all things. There's no shortcut to knowing Christ.

Prayer

God, help me make you the most important pursuit in my life. I know what it's like to pursue fishing and hunting with zeal and enthusiasm. Please help me chase after you with even greater purpose and sacrifice. I need your Spirit's help in this ongoing work. Amen.

69

THE SURVIVAL WORD

Scripture Passage: *"The LORD has made everything for its purpose, even the wicked for the day of trouble."* —Proverbs 16:4

READ: EPHESIANS 1:3–14

If you hunt or fish in dangerous country such as Alaska or northern Canada, you need to carry a survival pack—a bag with water, food, matches, and various other necessities. You can go almost anywhere if you have this well-prepared survival pack strapped to your back.

In a similar way, God's sovereignty, which describes God's perfect governance over all things in heaven and on earth, helps our faith survive anything we go through in life. Here are a few verses that teach us that God is in complete control over all things:

> For kingship belongs to the LORD, and he rules over the nations. (Ps. 22:28)

> But he is unchangeable, and who can turn him back? What he desires, that he does. (Job 23:13)

> For his dominion is an everlasting dominion, and his kingdom endures from generation to generation; all the inhabitants of the earth are accounted as nothing, and he does according to his will among the host of heaven and among the inhabitants of the earth; and none can stay his hand or say to him, "What have you done?" (Dan. 4:34–35)

When we understand and believe in the sovereignty of God, we carry a rock-solid confidence that nothing happens to us that doesn't come from the hands of our loving Father. This idea is perfectly captured in Romans 8:28: "And we know that for those who love God all things work together for good, for those who are called according to his purpose."

There is certainly a mystery to God's sovereignty. Though he is not the author or agent behind moral evil, nothing wicked happens in this life that God doesn't permit for the good of those who love him. There is also a mystery to how God allows us the freedom to make choices and experience consequences, yet his sovereignty isn't compromised or lessened by our choices—it is carried out through them.

When we understand this much about the sovereignty of God, we are ready to walk with faith, hope, and love through any situation in life. Whether we are fired or promoted, we can know God is in control. Whether we have children or remain childless, God is perfect in his governance. Whether we live the life we always dreamed we'd live or something radically different, God is good and is accomplishing precisely what he wants to in us.

Trying to journey through life without this truth would be like going into the wild without any provisions. Our faith simply would not survive trials without knowing God is sovereign. The theologian B. B. Warfield attested to this. On his honeymoon, lightning struck his wife, paralyzing her. Warfield cared for his bride for the next thirty-nine years. As he reflected on Romans 8:28, he wrote:

> If He governs all, then nothing but good can befall those to whom He would do good. . . . Though we are too weak to help ourselves and too blind to ask for what we need, and can only groan in unformed longings, He is the author in us of these very longings . . . and He will so govern all things that we shall reap only good from all that befalls us.[1]

Prayer

Father, help me trust you no matter what comes into or goes out of my life. I believe that you are sovereignly in control of all things, so please help me practice this belief in my everyday ups and downs. Produce joy in my heart, Father, from knowing you are causing all things to work together for my good. Amen.

1. Benjamin B. Warfield, *Faith and Life* (Edinburgh: Banner of Truth, 1991), 20.

70

THE JEALOUS LOVE
OF GOD

Scripture Passage: *"You shall not bow down to them or serve them, for I the LORD your God am a jealous God, visiting the iniquity of the fathers on the children to the third and the fourth generation of those who hate me, but showing steadfast love to thousands of those who love me and keep my commandments."* —Exodus 20:5–6

READ: HOSEA 3

Shortly after moving to central Nebraska, I got invited to join a friend in a pit blind along the Platte River. When we reached the enclosure, the owner of the blind slid the door open, welcomed us into the bunker, and handed us a plate of bacon, eggs, and hash browns. One of the other hunters shook my hand, then pointed to a stack of pornographic magazines on a shelf and said, "Help yourself! Just don't let God see you."

We often fail to appreciate the *true* problem of sin. We tend to think that God is most concerned with our behaviors and actions. We think God is most disappointed in us when we look at porn, steal money, or lie to our spouse. This is shortsighted. Actions and behaviors do matter to God, but only because they spring from our hearts. Our affections, motivations, and devotions—those things that reveal our hearts—are what concern God the most.

Few books of the Bible make this point more colorfully than the book of Hosea. This small Old Testament book presents a vital picture of the zealous, jealous love of God. At the time, Israel was involved in numerous sins, many of which were sexual and involved worshiping false idols. God wanted to show his people that what he cared about the most was their heart's orientation toward him. To do this, God commanded a prophet, Hosea, to marry a prostitute, Gomer. This was a scandal of epic proportions—a faithful, holy man of God marrying an unclean, idolatrous woman who had sex with multiple men. Once married, Hosea and Gomer enjoy marriage for a season. They have a son, Jezreel, and then Hosea begins to notice a change in Gomer. She starts to feel pangs of restlessness and discontent. She wanders from the marriage, ends up pregnant again, but this time it's not Hosea's child. The pattern of unfaithfulness continues throughout this prophetic book, and Hosea is agonized. And all Israel is swept up in the scandal, sympathizing with Hosea's plight.

God used Hosea's pain as a living word picture to show his people that he expects their full devotion and loyalty, much like a husband expects this from his wife. Our sinful actions do matter because they reveal that our hearts are not fully committed to the God who loves us. When we who claim to walk by faith in Jesus treasure certain sins, we are committing adultery in our hearts against our true love, God. Through Hosea's pain, God shows us that he expects to be at the very center of our heart, holding our deepest affections and loyalties. He's jealous for our devotion, in part because he knows we will only find our deepest satisfaction and pleasure in him.

When the goose hunter offered me porn, it took me a few moments to figure out how to respond. I didn't want to sound preachy or self-righteous, so I simply said, "Thanks, but I'm going to pass. God can see everything, including my heart."

The man scrunched up his face as if he was confused, or at least not convinced. He asked, "Do you really believe that? Do you really think God cares about what's going on in our hearts?"

I replied, "You bet. When it comes to people, there's nothing he cares about more."

Prayer

Holy Spirit, please show me if there is anything in my heart that I am treasuring above Christ. If I have an idol or false love, please convict me of it, and then help me to return to the Lord and give him my pure devotion and loyalty. Help me enjoy your reckless, raging love above all things in life. Amen.

71

Hating Our Hate

Scripture Passage: *"Be angry and do not sin; do not let the sun go down on your anger, and give no opportunity to the devil."* —Ephesians 4:26–27

READ: ROMANS 12:17–21

Rick Garmon took his gun out of the cabinet, cleaned it, and prepared it for use. He wasn't going hunting. He wasn't going out to the range to shoot targets. Rick was planning to shoot the man who had raped his eighteen-year-old daughter. Katie was a freshman in college when she was raped on a date. She withdrew from life, trying to hide the incident and the pain. When Rick found out about this crime, he began plotting a way to end the life of the man who had taken so much away from Katie.

Garmon's son, Thomas, came downstairs while Rick was cleaning the gun and thinking of revenge. His son asked him what he was doing, and Rick realized that if he carried out his plan, Thomas would not have a father. Rick says, "Locking the gun in the cabinet, I made a choice to forgive. God, I gotta let go of this hate. It's killing me."[1]

When we hold on to our anger and hate, we are committing homicide of the heart—our own heart. Nothing has the power to destroy our lives like the desire to take vengeance into our own hands and make others pay for what they've done to us. When God tells us, "Vengeance is mine, I will repay" (Rom. 12:19), he's telling us to trust that he sees perfectly, and one day he will set all things right. We don't have absolute vision, so when we take matters into our own hands and hurt those who hurt us, we execute judgment imperfectly. When we turn an offender over to God for him to

1. Rick Garmon, "My Secret Hate," as told to Julie West Garmon, Crosswalk. com, May 1, 2006, http://www.crosswalk.com/11622668/.

IN PURSUIT

judge, we are heaping "burning coals on his head" (Rom. 12:20). "Burning coals" represents punishment or discipline that fits the offense. When we love, serve, and pray for those who offend us, in our hearts we place the offender into the Lord's hands. We can know that he will deal with that person in perfect justice.

Loving those who hurt us is impossibly hard to do in our own strength. Whether it's an unfaithful spouse, a lying friend, a controlling parent, or, as in Rick Garmon's situation, someone who hurts a person we deeply care about, we need the grace and help of God to overcome evil with good. But God gives this grace and help every time we need it; we just need to ask him for it. When God opened Rick's eyes to see the foolishness of his plan to kill the man who raped his daughter, Rick prayed and confessed his anger. He also told his wife about his intentions, and they prayed together. Surrendering the offense to God and asking God for help made Rick alive again.

What anger and hate have you been holding onto? You don't have to carry it anymore. Turn the offense over to the God who judges and punishes all wickedness. When vengeance is his, rest will be yours. It's time to rest, my friend.

Prayer

Jesus, I know that anger and resentment can eat me alive on the inside. Please help me release my strong feelings to you. I know that you see everything and will judge perfectly—help me trust you with the things that are most upsetting me today. Free my heart to love, Jesus. Amen.

72

RULE BREAKERS

Scripture Passage: *"But sin, seizing an opportunity through the commandment, produced in me all kinds of covetousness. For apart from the law, sin lies dead."* —Romans 7:8

READ: ROMANS 7:7–12

We are rule breakers, but without rules we might not know this about ourselves. To illustrate this point, Haddon Robinson tells a story about a hotel in Texas that was built on a pier overlooking the Gulf of Mexico:

> When the hotel was about to have its grand opening, someone thought, "What if people decide to fish out the hotel windows?" So they placed signs in the hotel rooms, "No fishing out the hotel windows." Many people ignored the signs, however, and it created a difficult problem. Lines got snarled. People in the dining room saw fish flapping against the picture windows. The manager of the hotel solved it all by taking down those little signs. No one checks into a hotel room thinking about fishing out of the windows. The law, although well intentioned, created the problem.[1]

When God gave Moses the law at Mount Sinai, he gave the entire world knowledge about what is right and what is wrong. The law of God shows us what God defines as sin. But it does more than just describe sin. The law interacts with our hearts and provokes us to sin, as Romans 7:5 points out: "For while we were living in the flesh, our sinful passions, aroused by the law, were at work in our members to bear fruit for death." The fact that the law arouses sin in us doesn't mean that the law itself is sinful or evil.

IN PURSUIT

1. Haddon Robinson, *Biblical Preaching: The Development and Delivery of Expository Messages*, 2nd ed. (Grand Rapids: Baker Academic, 2001), 100.

The commands that God gives us in his Word are holy, revealing truths about the character of God and what he desires from us. However, when the law of God connects with a heart bent toward rebellion, it stimulates sin within that heart. As the apostle Paul admitted, "For I would not have known what it is to covet if the law had not said, 'You shall not covet.' But sin, seizing an opportunity through the commandment, produced in me all kinds of covetousness" (Rom. 7:7–8).

One of the many reasons why we read the Bible is that it shows us what God expects us to do in order to gain eternal life. To be with God, we need to be righteous and perfect; the law of God spells out what righteousness and perfection look like. When we read the Bible and see the holiness God expects, we rightly feel desperate about our prospects. "There's no way I can live up to God's expectations," is an appropriate response when we understand the law. In fact, our sense of inadequacy is vital to our accepting that the gospel of God's grace is truly *good news*. When we see that we are rule breakers who fall short of the glory of God, we are ready to receive the righteousness and perfection God offers those who place their faith in Jesus.

Do you ever feel like fishing from a hotel window when there is a sign that says "No fishing out the hotel windows"? Do you find yourself breaking the commands and precepts of God as soon as you become aware of them? This points to your need for grace and his moment-by-moment gift of forgiveness and righteousness through his Son, Jesus. Let the commands and the convictions that follow drive you to Christ. That's their purpose.

Prayer

Jesus, thank you for living the perfect life that I could not live. Thank you for keeping the law of God to the letter, and then giving me your righteousness by grace through faith. By your Spirit, help me live a holy life—not because I have to in order to measure up but because I get to by your power and grace. Amen.

73

A HERITAGE OF BUSYNESS

Scripture Passage: *"For we hear that some among you are leading an undisciplined life, doing no work at all, but acting like busybodies."* —2 Thessalonians 3:11 NASB

READ: LUKE 10:38–42

As a father, I'm thinking a lot these days about what I'm passing on to my children. A conversation I had with my friend Doug a few weeks ago reminded me of the importance of this time with my children still at home. Doug and I had been playing basketball with a handful of guys. After the game, the two of us sat on the bottom step of the bleachers and talked about basketball injuries until the last guy left the gym. When we had the place to ourselves, Doug hung his head. He explained how his son, Todd, a freshman in college, hadn't returned his phone calls for a couple weeks.

Doug started to cry a bit, and I began to wonder if this guy who could throw an elbow with the best of them was, in fact, an overly sensitive man; I'd never heard a father cry over his son not returning his calls. Then he explained, "It's not that Todd hasn't called. What's tearing me up is that I had my son under my roof for eighteen years, and the main thing I taught him was how to stay busy. All he does is hang out with friends, play video games, and work to make money to pay for his parties."

Todd's eighteen years in the home coincided with the critical years of Doug's ascent up the corporate ladder. Doug worked late most nights. He also signed his children up for every sport their town offered. Weekends became about which parent would shuttle which child to the ballet recital or baseball tournament. Doug described how their family of five would go months at a time without having a slow, uninterrupted dinner together. They missed church most Sundays, didn't join Bible studies, didn't help to meet the needs of those in their community. Doug said, "For eighteen years, I told myself it was just a season. But things never slowed down. I passed on a heritage of busyness to my son."

It is possible for us to be busy but unproductive. Paul calls such people "idle busybodies." These are people who run at a fast pace, involving themselves in numerous activities, but without contributing in a meaningful way to their community. They work and play hard, and life feels perpetually fast-paced and filled up, but they aren't actually being productive. An idle busybody passes on a partially developed sense of self to his children. As Dallas Willard writes, "Marching onward in life, these little people become big people and move on with their malfunctioning souls into workplace, profession, citizenship, and leadership. From them proceeds the next generation of wounded souls."[1]

It's not wrong to work and play hard, but as men we must prioritize our time according to our commitments to people in our spiritual community and town or city. A well-formed heart knows how to work and have fun, but it also knows how to read, rest, relax, think, reflect, and make intentional decisions. It knows how to meet the real and obvious need of our neighbors. It knows how to be more than busy. Is your heart well formed by the grace of God? Everyone in your life needs that answer to be yes.

Prayer

Father, help me live an intentional, focused life today so that my children gain a vision for living such a life tomorrow. I want to hand off a heritage of godliness and faith, Father. I need your help to do this. Help me rely on your Spirit to make good choices and choose the best priorities. Amen.

1. Dallas Willard, *Renovation of the Heart: Putting on the Character of Christ* (Colorado Springs: NavPress, 2002), 192.

74

HUMPTY DUMPTY
WASN'T BROKEN

Scripture Passage: *"The LORD is near to the broken-hearted and saves the crushed in spirit."*—Psalm 34:18

READ: PSALM 51

There are two kinds of brokenness: the type that poor ol' Mr. Dumpty experienced when he took a tumble and cracked his shell, and the type that the Bible describes. As Christians, we often confuse these ideas.

I once hunted turkey with a friend who was going through a challenging season. He was in a new management position, and many of his employees were bucking his authority. Some of his investments had recently taken a beating, and he was feeling the financial strain. He'd been struggling with a long-term sickness that had him feeling tired and worn out every day. When he finished giving me the update on his difficulties, he said, "I'm just so broken, Zeke."

My friend was using the Humpty definition, referring to his weariness as "brokenness." But according to the Scriptures, to be broken means to be brokenhearted about our sins. When Nathan rebuked King David for his sins involving Bathsheba and Uriah, David replied, "I have sinned against the LORD" (2 Sam. 12:13). David went to his house and fasted, wept, and prayed. He composed Psalm 51, which is a poem of true brokenness. In that psalm, David admits his sin, asks God for mercy, and desires nothing more than to be made clean by God's grace.

There is tremendous power and beauty that follows biblical brokenness. When a man understands the evil in his heart and feels appropriately humble and contrite about it, he's ever so near to the grace and mercy of God. And the experience of grace and mercy always changes a man. When King David owned his sin, confessed, and placed himself into the forgiving hands of God, God lifted him up. Psalm 51:12 records David's plea for God to "restore to me the joy of your salvation, and uphold me with a willing spirit." God did just that for David, and David was forever changed. He remained the king of Israel, leading his people with a humility and strength he didn't have before he was broken.

Are you aware of sin in your life? Let me encourage you to ask God for help in feeling the appropriate brokenness. And when that conviction comes, ask him for forgiveness and restoration. Nobody could heal Humpty Dumpty from his type of brokenness, but God promises to restore the contrite man from his.

Prayer

Father, help me have such a clear picture of your holiness and perfection that it continues to show me my need for grace. When I sin, convict me by your Spirit and bring me to repentance. Help me experience the depth of brokenness that David experienced when he sinned against you with Bathsheba. I want to be a man after your own heart. Amen.

75

YOU BE THE JUDGE

Scripture Passage: *"Brothers, if anyone is caught in any transgression, you who are spiritual should restore him in a spirit of gentleness. Keep watch on yourself, lest you too be tempted."* —Galatians 6:1

READ: MATTHEW 7:1–5

Mark did something unethical a few years ago when he let another deer hunter fill his landowner tag. He told his buddy to shoot another buck and then give him a call. Mark said, "I'll drive out into the field and we can put my tag around its antlers." Another sportsman in our community, Daniel, heard about Mark's strategy and called him on it. Mark responded to Daniel's criticism, saying, "You Christians are all the same. Jesus even said, 'Judge not, that you be not judged.'" Healthy, encouraging friendships require that men make judgments about one another. This idea flies in the face of popular opinion today.

Mark applied Jesus's words incorrectly. Jesus was not telling us to remain silent when a friend does something wrong. He was telling us to pay particularly close attention to whether or not *we* are doing something wrong. Jesus wasn't condemning all judgments, rebukes, and corrections between friends; he was speaking against a haughty, prideful attitude that prevents us from also recognizing our own sins and shortcomings. A few verses later, Jesus said, "You hypocrite, first take the log out of your own eye, and then you will see clearly to take the speck out of your brother's eye" (Matt. 7:5).

When people care about one another, they play an active role in one another's lives. If a man makes a decision to obey God, his friends should notice, judge the decision, and cheer him on. However, if the same man chooses the wrong path and sins against God, his closest friends should notice, judge the decision, and rebuke his

IN PURSUIT

168

sin. Loving one another involves making accurate judgments about one another. A loving wife discerns her husband's words and actions, then gently encourages him or corrects him, depending on what she sees. Healthy churches are filled with people who make good judgments, and occasionally they have to take a person through the painful but necessary process of church discipline. A judgment is simply an assessment of what is right and what is wrong. The Scriptures command us to do this for one another in love.

If we love each other, we will talk about sin. We will first look into our own lives to see what needs to be confessed or corrected. But we'll also humbly help our wives, children, and brothers in Christ look into theirs. Jesus said that the truth will set us free, so our desire for freedom will compel us to action.

When Mark attacked Daniel for challenging him on his plan to share a tag with another hunter, Daniel pushed back. He looked Mark squarely in the eye and said, "What kind of a friend would I be if I didn't encourage you to do the right thing?"

Mark thought about that for a moment, took a deep breath, and said, "You know . . . you're right. And don't ever quit telling me the truth. I need a friend like you." We all do.

Prayer

Jesus, help me be a good friend by making accurate judgments. Please give me a keen eye to recognize the sin in my own life, and give me the wisdom to see sin and righteousness in other people's lives, as well. Help me have the courage to say something when necessary. Amen.

76

SHAKING THINGS UP

Scripture Passage: *"One thing I do know, that though I was blind, now I see."* —John 9:25

READ: JOHN 9

Last year I spoke at a funeral for an older sportsman who had died in a small town in Nebraska. During my message, I mentioned that God has the power to change people's lives in dramatic ways, day in and day out. After the funeral, a friend and hunting buddy of the deceased came up to me and said, "I've never really believed in God, but I think I'd like to. I'd just need to see him do something big and dramatic in my life."

"Be careful what you wish for," I replied. And then I told him about a blind man in John's Gospel. Jesus performed a miracle on his behalf, and it flipped his entire world upside down.

In the ancient Middle Eastern culture of Jesus's day, poor people played an important role. Every religious, upstanding member of the community was expected to give money to the poor. Giving alms, or gifts to the poor, was a way that people tried to prove their righteousness. Traditionally, when a wealthy person threw money into a blind person's cup, the blind would yell in their loudest voice that a generous person had just given them money. All eyes would turn, and the benefactor would gain a sense of self-worth and public acclaim from the attention. The poor would get money, and the wealthy would get fame. As twisted and broken as this system was, it benefited both parties.

Then Jesus performed a miracle and changed everything in a blind man's life. When Jesus saw a man who had been blind since birth, he spit in the dirt, made mud, and wiped the mud on the man's eyes. When the man washed the mud away, he could see. For the first time in his life, he saw colors, shapes, and faces to go along with voices. But when he gained his sight, he lost his income. This free gift Jesus gave the blind beggar was extremely costly. With no disability, there would be no offerings. He didn't have a job. He didn't have an education. He didn't have skills, training, or a network of support in any way. He had gained his sight, but lost almost everything else familiar and safe in his life. What's more, the religious leaders who hated Jesus now hated the former blind man. They kicked him out of the synagogue, which effectively meant this man was booted from society. At the end of the story, Jesus finds the man again and asks him, "Do you believe in the Son of Man?" (John 9:35). The man admits that he does, and then he worships Jesus, enjoying being in the presence of the God of all creation.

There is no greater pleasure in life than to know God. The psalmist says, "In [God's] presence there is fullness of joy; at [his] right hand are pleasures forevermore" (Ps. 16:11). The more we trust in God and follow his ways, the more joy and pleasure we will experience. Yet, this doesn't mean that things in life will get easier. The God who changed reality for the blind man still shakes things up in our lives today.

At the end of our discussion, the man at the funeral replied, "I'll have to think about this Jesus character. If I'm hearing you right, it sounds like following him could lead to huge changes. And some might be very difficult."

I replied, "Now you're getting it. That's the life of faith."

Prayer

Father, I realize that you are powerful, and that when you do your work in my life, things will change. Please accomplish your purposes for me, making me more like Jesus and teaching me to trust you more each day. Help me walk by grace through whatever new experiences—hard or easy—you bring. Amen.

77

GIT 'ER DONE

Scripture Passage: *"I love those who love me, and those who seek me diligently find me."* —Proverbs 8:17

READ: JAMES 1:22–25

The hunting and fishing worlds are filled with extremely passionate, dedicated men. Very few people limp into these sports; they're all in or all out. They read magazines, watch outdoor shows, attend trade shows, and flip slowly and methodically through their favorite product catalogs. All this interaction is driven by the desire to improve and find more success in the field or on the water. As sportsmen interact with all this information, they scrutinize their own practices, adjust their strategies, and employ the best equipment possible. Improvement leads to greater accomplishment.

The same is true in our relationship with God. If we would apply the same examination, reflection, and commitment to action in our spiritual lives, we would enter new territory. The book of James contains the promise that if a man hears the Word of God, examines his life, and then puts God's truth into action, "he will be blessed in his doing" (James 1:25).

When we compare our motivation to enjoy outdoor hobbies with our motivation to grow in relationship with God, we often see a marked difference. While we have experienced firsthand the excitement of catching a fish or wrapping a tag around an impressive set of antlers, many of us have not experienced the exhilaration of the soul that comes from a sense that all is well between us and our Creator. I'm a sportsman who has felt the pleasures of a successful day outside. I've also experienced the enjoyment of growing in my faith and knowledge of God. And I can say with full conviction, there is simply no comparison—the pursuit of God in spirit and in truth is far more exhilarating.

May we sportsmen remain passionate about our outdoor pursuits. Hunting and fishing are great endeavors that provide time with friends and family, opportunities to appreciate God's creation, and food for our tables. Such activities are worth our energy and commitment. But may we not forget that we were created to satisfy the heart's *strongest* desires in the person of Jesus Christ. To pursue and apprehend Jesus, we must apply the same diligence of study and commitment to growth that we bring to our sports.

God promises to be found by the man who is truly pursuing him. Hunters and fishermen know what it means to seek diligently. May our best passion and zeal be directed toward the pursuit of God. It's the adventure our souls were made for.

Prayer

Father, help me know and obey your Word. I want to go "all in" when it comes to my relationship with you. Give me a passion for walking with you that is even greater than my passion for spending time outside. You are the source of life, and I want to experience the blessings of knowing you. Amen.

78

KEEP IT SIMPLE

Scripture Passage: *"I perceived that there is nothing better for them than to be joyful and to do good as long as they live; also that everyone should eat and drink and take pleasure in all his toil—this is God's gift to man."* —Ecclesiastes 3:12–13

READ: ECCLESIASTES 3:1-13

As I'm writing today, a new season is sweeping into central Nebraska. Everything that was verdant and bustling with life is dead or dormant. The deer are losing their antlers, the wild turkeys are clustered into large groups, and enormous flocks of Canada geese are flying past our house in search of warmer weather to the south. The leaves are gone. The orioles and yellow finches that flittered and filled our backyard with song have left. Even the cornstalks that hemmed us in on all four sides have been picked, chopped, and tilled under. Our acreage feels exposed on the vast, vulnerable prairie.

And yet, we have a fire in the fireplace every night. Hot drinks taste better after shoveling snow and splitting wood in cold, crisp air. We're bringing the dogs in more often at night, letting them sit on their places at the hearth and adding warmth and pleasure to the living room. There are large pots of venison stew, and friends stop by to enjoy the fire and soup with us. And there's also the anticipation of spring, its gift of green still a few months away, and the reminder that a new fishing and hunting season is on the horizon. I have sharply mixed feelings about this time of year.

We were created for the seasons. Ecclesiastes 3, one of my favorite passages in the Bible, celebrates this fact. It also points to the reality that life is short and fleeting, and that the next season, eternal life, is right around the corner. Solomon, the author of

Ecclesiastes, reflects on all living things when he writes, "All go to one place. All are from the dust, and to dust all return" (3:20).

If you are reading this devotion, you are, quite obviously, alive. But for how long? Nobody knows, including you. And the day will come when you and I, we who hunt and fish on this earth right now, will turn back into the dust of the ground. In 120 years, every person on the earth will be gone and several new generations of life will have taken over. There is humility in coming to grips with this, and it is vitally healthy.

After reflecting on the seasons of life and death, Solomon's conclusion is, "Fear God and keep his commandments, for this is the whole duty of man" (Eccles. 12:13). Enjoy your work. Enjoy your family and friends. Enjoy hunting, fishing, hiking, and exploring God's creation. But most of all, fear God and keep his commandments. Enjoy your Creator and live in the grace he has shown you in his Son, Jesus. This is a surprisingly simple vision for life coming from the man who made his own life so complex by accumulating land, wealth, women, and fame. In the end, Solomon learned that these worldly pursuits were vain and empty. Life and its various seasons remind us of one great priority: keep it simple.

Prayer

Father, thank you for how you created life to move in seasons. Help me appreciate the brevity of my life here on earth, and teach me how important it is to use these days to prepare for eternity with you. Help me enjoy my work, my family, my friends, and my life. Help me treasure you above all these good things. Amen.

79

ALL IN

Scripture Passage: *"You shall love the Lord your God with all your heart and with all your soul and with all your mind."* —Matthew 22:37

READ: MATTHEW 4:18–22

Although their fishing methods were different, I can relate to Simon and Andrew. These brothers spent most days untangling lines, freeing up snags, and trying to keep their catch alive until they could haul it back to shore. And then one day, a Jewish carpenter-turned-rabbi strolled along the shoreline and stopped within shouting distance of these men. He watched them fish for a moment, then called out, "Follow me, and I will make you fishers of men" (Matt. 4:19).

This was an extraordinary moment on an otherwise ordinary day. Jewish rabbis didn't invite fishermen to follow them as disciples. Rabbis were revered and admired; they could handpick the best and brightest young Hebrew scholars. Simon and Andrew, given the fact that they were tradesmen, were clearly far from the best and brightest. They didn't have the best pedigree, the best minds, or the best theology. They were ordinary men on course to take over their father's fishing business. Yet, Jesus invited them to be his disciples anyway. And, equally amazing, they took Jesus up on his offer. They left their father, family business, and way of life behind to follow Jesus and be his apprentices.

Sportsmen can appreciate this radical commitment. We know what it's like to pursue something with zeal and enthusiasm. We're famous (perhaps infamous) for throwing ourselves into fishing and hunting. We read magazines, set out trail cameras, fiddle with our gear, and lose ourselves for hours at a time in sporting goods stores. Few sportsmen engage their passion on a mediocre, passionless level. We're either all in, or not in at all.

This is the way of Christ. Jesus invites us to either follow him with all our heart, mind, soul, and strength . . . or not follow him at all. Some people live as if there is a third option of limping into this Christian life halfheartedly. According to God's Word, that's the one option that shouldn't be on the table. When Jesus criticized the church in Laodicea, he said, "I know your works: you are neither cold nor hot. Would that you were either cold or hot! So, because you are lukewarm, and neither hot nor cold, I will spit you out of my mouth" (Rev. 3:15–16).

Simon and Andrew made a radical commitment to follow Jesus as their rabbi. We have the same invitation and the same decision to make. The choice doesn't necessarily mean we need to quit our jobs, change our hobbies, or find new friends. However, the choice to say yes to Jesus as our rabbi is the choice to devote ourselves to pursuing him above all things. Simon and Andrew gave their very souls to Jesus. Will we do the same?

Prayer

Jesus, help me understand what it means to be your disciple. By your Spirit, give me the faith and spiritual resources I need to follow you and become more like you in my thoughts, feelings, and actions. Amen.

80

CHOPPING THE HEAD
OFF SIN

Scripture Passage: *"For if you live according to the flesh you will die, but if by the Spirit you put to death the deeds of the body, you will live."* —Romans 8:13

READ: ROMANS 8:12–17

I'm not sure that I've heard of a more difficult way to make money. My friend Doug captures rattlesnakes in the desert and sells their skins and rattles. He walks slowly across the sand, looking under rocks and sagebrush, locating rattlesnake dens. When he finds a snake, he grabs it by the tail and flings it onto the sand in front of the den before the snake has a chance to strike. Once the snake is out in the open, Doug pins it down and chops its head off.

Doug has always been faster than the snake. Except the one time he wasn't. It was a massive snake, approximately five feet long, and Doug was in the process of grabbing its tail when the rattler flung its head forward and struck him between his thumb and index finger. Forty blood transfusions and three weeks later, Doug was released from the hospital.

All of us have sin, even those who have put our faith in Jesus and try our best to walk by grace through faith. We still mess up. We still have addictions. We still make choices to disobey the God who created us. Our sin is our enemy, slithering under a rock, stealing our joy, and hurting our nearness to God. When we give in to sin, we die. When we put sin to death, we live. The apostle Paul writes, "For if you live according to the flesh you will die, but if by the Spirit you put to death the deeds of the body, you will live" (Rom. 8:13).

Let me suggest three simple steps toward putting sin to death: First, we must believe that sin and our sinful nature are already dead within us. Second Corinthians 5:17 reminds us that, "If anyone is in Christ, he is a new creation. The old has passed away; behold, the new has come." The *old* is referring to our spiritually dead state before Jesus gave us new life. Those who walk by faith must reckon that sin no longer reigns in us; it has been put to death by the work of Christ.

Second, we must view sin as something that steals life. If we hold out the slightest hope that sin might add pleasure or exhilaration to life, we will not kill it. I had a man once tell me in a counseling session, "I know I shouldn't look at pornography, but it's just that it makes me feel alive inside, even if it makes me feel bad later." We will not kill our close companions; if we don't view sin as our enemy, we will not take the knife to its throat.

Third, we must choose to walk in the grace of God. Grace is not permission to mess up or sin. Grace is not sweeping addictions and shortcomings under the table. Grace is not license. Grace is the free gift that God gives us of being completely forgiven and perfectly righteous because of Jesus. The more we believe the grace of God, the more hideous sin becomes. As the great old hymn "I Need Thee Every Hour" celebrates, "Temptations lose their power when Thou art nigh."

We cannot pull ourselves up by our own bootstraps and over-come a temptation or an addiction in our own strength. When we play around with sin, we're as good as dead. It's only by living in the grace of God that we will choose not to play with snakes in the first place.

Prayer

Father, I don't always take sin seriously or recognize its life-stealing power in my life. Help me sense conviction from your Spirit for my sins. Help me quickly come to you, confess my sins, and walk in your grace and forgiveness. I want to kill the sin in my body, and I need your help, Father. Amen.

81

HOLD THE CREAM CHEESE

Scripture Passage: *"Truly, I say to you, today you will be with me in Paradise."* —Luke 23:43

READ: REVELATION 21

Sportsmen are invigorated by the feeling of a current pressing in as we cast our fly toward cool, dark pools near the river's bank. The smell of cedar as we sit twenty feet off the ground waiting for an unsuspecting deer to take the trail we're watching puts a sense of life into us. Rocks, mountains, trees, brush, water, and all things wild make us feel alive inside. Our happiest, most energizing moments happen when we're in direct contact with the physical world.

So it's no wonder sportsmen often hold no enthusiasm toward the idea of heaven as popular culture usually presents it. If your vision of heaven is formed from movies and commercials, you probably envision people floating from cloud to cloud, eating cream cheese, and listening to ethereal harp music. I'll be the first to admit, that picture of heaven holds as much power to inspire me as a cup of warm Kool-Aid.

Thankfully, heaven is nothing like what popular culture has dreamed up. For example, Jesus promised that it would be a place of feasting. He told his disciples during the Last Supper, "I tell you I will not drink again of this fruit of the vine until that day when I drink it new with you in my Father's kingdom" (Matt. 26:29). God promises that we will have bodies that are spiritual, but also physical and recognizable. Jesus, when he appeared in his resurrected body, invited his disciples to touch his hands and side. And God promises that when he returns, we will live with him on the earth. It will be a resurrected and redeemed earth, but it will be the same earth nonetheless. According to Revelation 21 and 22, the place where we will spend eternity will have trees, cities, and animals. It will even have rivers, and I have no reason to give up the hope that the River of Life contains unimaginably large and colorful trout.

Many sportsmen feel a sense of nearness to God and his creation when we're outdoors. This will not change for those who are in Christ when they die and enter life eternal. If anything, I suspect that redeemed rivers flow more fiercely, resurrected mountains contain sharper peaks, and renewed forests teem with larger, healthier animals. I imagine the whitetail's tail is whiter, the rainbow trout more colorful, and the black bear's coat blacker than a lump of coal. The more we understand Jesus's resurrected body, the more we are able to understand a physical resurrection of the earth.

Heaven isn't life in the clouds; it's life in a physical place, with trees, rivers, mountains, and prairies. Randy Alcorn writes, "Just like the Garden of Eden, the New Earth will be a place of sensory delight, breathtaking beauty, satisfying relationships, and personal joy."[1] This is heaven according to the Scriptures. And this is something all sportsmen can get excited about.

Prayer

God, please give me a huge, beautiful, accurate picture of heaven from your Word. I want to look forward to life after death, and I trust you that it will be even more exhilarating and pleasurable than life right now. Please fill out my picture of heaven so that it is a deeply motivating and encouraging vision. Amen.

1. Randy Alcorn, *Heaven* (Wheaton: Tyndale, 2004), 241.

82

KINGDOM INVESTMENTS

Scripture Passage: *"Where your treasure is, there your heart will be also."* —Matthew 6:21

READ: HEBREWS 13:5–6

What we spend our money on reveals the affections of our heart. But how we spend our resources also cultivates affections that might not be present yet. For example, I recently purchased a revolver for home defense. Before purchasing it, I didn't know or care much about handguns. A few of my close friends have owned revolvers for years, but I'd never desired to hold or shoot them. Revolvers meant nothing to me. Until . . . I put my money toward a short-nosed .357, a holster, and a handgun safety class. Now I'm very interested in revolvers, and I pay close attention when I see one in a store, in a movie, or on the belt of a law enforcement officer. I also care more deeply about gun legislation than I did before purchasing a gun. How we spend our money helps determine the direction of our heart.

Jesus said, "Where your treasure is, there your heart will be also" (Matt. 6:21). This truth applies to every area of our lives. If we have to work hard and save money in order to purchase a house, we will care more about our home than if the government or a wealthy relative simply gave it to us. As sportsmen, part of the reason we have such a deep interest in hunting and fishing is that we have invested so much time, attention, and money into these hobbies. Our money and time go to the things we care about, but they also direct where our passion resides. What starts out as a love for these great sports deepens into a passion over time as we pour in more of our resources.

As a pastor, I can tell a lot about a man's heart by how he spends his money. It always shocks the man who comes in for counseling when I ask to view his checkbook register. My reason for doing that is we can spend fifty hours talking about his life and priorities, but I still won't know his heart as well as if I could spend fifteen minutes looking at his credit card statements and checkbook.

I often have people tell me that they want to love God more, or value the things of heaven more than the things of earth. People usually make these statements with an air of sadness, assuming they have no control over their affections and treasures. Yet, Jesus's words tell us otherwise. If we want to love God more, then we ought to invest in his work and his kingdom. If we want to care more about world missions, then we ought to write more checks to missions agencies or take more flights to visit missionaries in the field. If we want to value the poor, the orphans, the widows, the sick, the incarcerated, then we ought to pull out our checkbooks and calendars and invest money and time.

Let me encourage you to study your checkbook and credit card statements; examine your heart by looking at your spending over the past three months. There's nothing inherently wrong about investing in a truck, a hunting lease, or a new revolver. Our possessions are valuable, but we must not let them become the most important things in our lives. If all of our resources are going to playthings, our heart is not going to form properly. Aleksandr Solzhenitsyn wisely writes, "We always pay dearly for chasing after what is cheap."[1]

If you want your heart to change, grow, and develop a kingdom-oriented passion, Jesus gives us a very simple starting point: begin investing your time and money into the things of God, and you can expect your heart to follow.

Prayer

Father, give me a heart that is sold out and committed to your purposes. Help me spend and invest my money and resources in your kingdom, even making foolish decisions in the world's eyes to serve you and advance your purposes. Help me view my money, time, and possessions from the perspective of eternity. Amen.

1. Aleksandr Solzhenitsyn, quoted in Randy Alcorn, *Money, Possessions, and Eternity* (Wheaton: Tyndale, 2003), 59.

83

FINDING RHYTHM

Scripture Passage: *"The lines have fallen for me in pleasant places; indeed, I have a beautiful inheritance. I bless the LORD who gives me counsel; in the night also my heart instructs me."* —Psalm 16:6–7

READ: JOHN 15:1–17

Fly-fishing is a sport of rhythm. There is a cadence to the cast, requiring the fisherman to feel and respond appropriately to the rod, line, fly on the water, and even the wind. There is also a harmony between the fly tied to the end of the tippet and the insects that are present in the stream. And there are flow rates and patterns to the river that must be understood by the angler. To have success, a fly fisherman must learn these rhythms and combine them with art and skill. As Norman Maclean writes in *A River Runs Through It*, "All good things—trout as well as eternal salvation—come by grace and grace by art and art does not come easy."[1]

Life as God created it also has rhythms; to live artfully and skillfully requires that we appreciate these rhythms. Jesus is the perfect example of a man who lived according to God's designs. We read about Jesus in the Gospels and think of him as God, which of course he is. But he was also fully human, and much of what we see in the Gospels shows us what we are capable of being if we will submit to God and be filled with the Spirit. When we look at Jesus's life, we see that he was fruitful because he remained close to his heavenly Father. He studied the Scriptures, spent time talking with and listening to his Father, and chose to obey his Father's commands. The Father knows his plans for all creation, and he knows us perfectly. If we remain close to him, we will live

1. Norman Maclean, *A River Runs Through It and Other Stories* (Chicago: University of Chicago Press, 1976), 4.

IN PURSUIT

with full confidence that he is with us, showing us his designs, purposes, and rhythms.

Shortly before he was executed, Jesus told his disciples that if they remained close to God, they would bear fruit: "I am the vine; you are the branches. Whoever abides in me and I in him, he it is that bears much fruit, for apart from me you can do nothing" (John 15:5). Jesus remained attuned to God's work in the world by remaining close to his Father. And we also live productive, fruitful lives by abiding in God. The pattern has not changed. Our Father in heaven wants us to bear fruit. He is glorified when we do. Jesus said, "*By* this my Father is glorified, that you bear much fruit and so prove to be my disciples" (John 15:8). God has great designs and plans for your life to be effective and rewarding. Your role in the process is to abide. Stay close to God, and he'll provide everything you need for the journey.

Prayer

Jesus, help me walk with you in a way that bears fruit. I want to think, feel, and act like you think, feel, and act. Help me seek you each day and find in you the rhythm for my life. Thank you for being a personal God who desires a close relationship with me. Amen.

84

SOUL TO SOUL

Scripture Passage: *"As soon as he had finished speaking to Saul, the soul of Jonathan was knit to the soul of David, and Jonathan loved him as his own soul."*
—1 Samuel 18:1

READ: 1 SAMUEL 18:1–5

David's friendship with Jonathan represents the type of brother-to-brother friendships that God created us to have. What made this famous friendship so unshakable was that the men shared the same convictions about the Lord. They knew that God was good, that he could be trusted, and that those who live to honor him will be victorious in the end. We know from his courage against Goliath that David's confidence was in the Lord, and we see this same faith in Jonathan when his father's army went up against the Philistines in 1 Samuel 14.

In March 2013, we saw a similar expression of friendship during the worst sports injury ever captured on television. As Louisville's Kevin Ware lay on the basketball court, six inches of leg bone protruding from his skin, his teammate Luke Hancock raced to his side. Hancock held Ware's hand and told him that they'd get through this together. He squeezed Ware's hand and started praying, "Lord, watch over us and let Kevin be okay during this tough time." Then he told his injured friend, "The Lord does everything for a reason, and He will get us through this."[1] After the prayer, Hancock continued to pat his friend's chest, telling him that he'd make it through this injury. The two stayed together until they took Ware off the court.

1. Adam Himmelsbach, "Kevin Ware on Louisville Teammate That 'Touched My Heart,'" *USA TODAY* online, April 4, 2013, http://www.usatoday.com/story/sports/ncaab/bigeast/2013/04/04/luke-hancock-kevin-ware-support-broken-leg/2052185/.

Life is hard. For all the pleasures we experience, the bone still breaks through the skin at times. Brotherhood is more than being a hunting or fishing buddy, although these sports can provide great opportunities to develop deeper bonds of trust. The key in transforming recreational friendship into a brotherhood for surviving life together is faith. Specifically, it's *sharing* faith together—talking with one another about trusting God, exhorting one other to take bold steps of obedience, and encouraging one another to live for Jesus when everything in the world encourages you to live for self. David and Jonathan shared a bold, courageous, unshakable faith in God. So did Luke and Kevin. And I'm thankful to say I have this shared faith with a few of my hunting and fishing comrades. These relationships are vital to the flourishing of my faith in Jesus.

Recently, my brother Bryan helped me walk through some challenges I was facing as a pastor. As we spent an evening on his bass pond, setting the hook on one largemouth after another, he listened to my situation, asked good questions, and then helped me think through what it could look like for me to walk by grace. I'm not sure how many fish we caught, but boating a bass was a secondary concern. The main thing I needed that day was encouragement and support as I tried to figure out what to do in order to be faithful. Bryan provided that for me—that's what brothers do.

And that's what you and your brothers can do for one another, if you'll talk openly about your hope and trust in God and commit to praying for one another. God can, and will, knit your souls together.

Prayer

Father, help me be the kind of friend that Jonathan was to David. Help me be quick to listen, quick to pray, and quick to act on behalf of my brothers in Christ. Father, please provide me with a friend who also trusts in you and who desires to be in my corner when life gets hard. Thank you for providing strength through my brothers. Amen.

85

THE STORM INSIDE

Scripture Passage: *"Whoever is slow to anger has great understanding, but he who has a hasty temper exalts folly."* —Proverbs 14:29

READ: COLOSSIANS 3:12–17

I used to be angry all the time. From about the time I was twelve until I turned twenty, I carried a chip on my shoulder the size of a trash can lid. Every car I owned in high school and college had dents on the dashboard that matched the knuckles on my fists. Wherever I went, I looked for a fight. A storm was always brewing on the inside, and it took very little to set off the thunder.

I see this same heart of anger in many men today. A few years back, I was hunting mule deer with a friend in New Mexico when two hunters stopped us on the path. One yelled, "You're hunting on *our* mountain! We've hunted this area since I was a kid. You out-of-state jerks think you own everything!" The heat from the man's face melted the snow on the pine trees as he continued his attack.

About twenty years ago, God used Colossians 3:12–17 to help replace my heart of anger with a heart of rest. I can remember the moment—it was during my sophomore year in college, and I was sitting at the hard, wooden desk in my dorm room. I'd placed my faith in Jesus a couple months before, but I was still an unstable hothead. And then I read about how I could choose to "put on" such virtues as "compassion, kindness, humility, meekness, and patience" (Col. 3:12). I realized that I had a choice to make: I could stay mad at the world, or I could let the grace of God seep into my heart and give me the resources to let go of my anger. This passage promises that when I choose to love others, "the peace of Christ" will rule in my heart (Col. 3:15). That's the beauty of obeying the command to "put on love"—it changed my experience of life. I no longer had to be compelled by anger or driven by a sense of inner chaos.

As a pastor, much of my time has been spent helping men release their anger and choose to love those who offend them. The way we do this is by reminding ourselves from the Scriptures of how much God has forgiven us. If anyone deserves to be angry, it's our Creator and heavenly Father. Yet, through the life and death of Jesus, he has satisfied his wrath and given us eternal life with him. When we begin to comprehend God's immeasurable mercy and love toward us, we gain the proper state of mind and heart. Christ becomes our vision for showing the mercy and grace of God toward others.

If you're one of the many men out there who have a storm brewing inside, and if the people around you often hear the thunder, let me encourage you to let it go. Pray and confess your anger as sin, and then ask God to replace your anger with the peace of Christ. Do this for others, but also do this for yourself. The inner calm that comes from putting on love will change your life. Take it from a man who, by the grace of God, hasn't hit a wall, a car dashboard, or a person since he was twenty. God *can* remove the storm inside.

Prayer

Father, forgive me for having a heart that is full of anger at times. I want to know your peace and joy, and I know that I must release my anger to experience them. Help me see and rejoice in the grace and mercy you have shown me. And then help me put on love toward others. Amen.

86

Gentle Men

Scripture Passage: *"Do not envy a man of violence
and do not choose any of his ways."* —Proverbs 3:31

READ: TITUS 3:1–11

Our culture is entertained by violence. The highest grossing video
games depict brutality with shocking realism. Many of the most
popular TV shows portray, with graphic detail, people getting killed
in psychotic ways. Even documentaries about animals are loaded
with scenes of fangs ripping flesh. Animals spend way more time
sleeping, pooping, and mating than they do killing; yet directors
know what consumers want, so they load up their programs with
entrails dangling from bloody mouths. Think for a moment of
what that says about us as a culture—we love watching beasts tear
up other beasts.

A sportsman doesn't need to turn in his "man card" in order to be
gentle. Quite the opposite. True masculinity involves men with great
strength of character exercising self-control, displaying kindness,
and using their power to protect and shelter the powerless. Some
men yell, throw things around, and make their presence known
because they think that's what it means to be tough. But there is
nothing manly or macho about being violent. Paul told Titus to
remind his church "to speak evil of no one, to avoid quarreling, to
be gentle, and to show perfect courtesy toward all people" (Titus
3:2). Few people were more courageous, bold, and driven than the
apostle Paul. He typifies a strong, biblical man, and he was kind,
gentle, and courteous.

Some may object to the idea that a sportsman can hate violence,
claiming that when a man pulls the trigger, releases the arrow, or
sets the hook, he's taking part in a violent act. But that point of
view fails to distinguish between what is necessary and what is

senseless. Hunting and fishing, although blood sports, enable us to acquire food for our families. We take responsibility for the life that has been sacrificed in order to meet our needs. It's not senseless as long as we respect our prey, make good use of the meat it provides, and remain sober about the act of taking a life.

In his poem "To Christ Our Lord," Galway Kinnell describes the appropriate reflection sportsmen often carry. "The Boy of the Far North" goes hunting in the snow and shoots a goose, then brings the bird home to cook for Christmas dinner. With his family around the table and the goose positioned between them, the boy becomes reflective. He thinks long and hard about the bird that died so his family could live. Kinnell writes about the boy, "He ate as he had killed, with wonder."[1]

A godly man uses his voice, presence, and physical strength to display concern and kindness to his community. He guards his eyes—those portals to his heart—from the violent images our culture uses to entertain. He realizes that the things that entertain him, form him; so he's selective about what he watches and celebrates.

Prayer

Father, help me not to desire or be entertained by violence. Help me guard my eyes and mind from evil things. Thank you, Lord, for the opportunity to fish and hunt as a means of providing food for my family and those in need. Yet, help me keep a sense of solemnity about the act of taking a life. Amen.

1. Galway Kinnell, *To Christ Our Lord* (West Chester, PA: Aralia Press, 1983).

87

Absolutely
Not Relative

Scripture Passage: *"If you abide in my word, you are truly my disciples, and you will know the truth, and the truth will set you free."* —John 8:31–32

Read: Psalm 119:153–160

"I finally shot the big one, Zeke. I'm on my way over to show you!"

Earl is sixty-seven years old and has been deer hunting for over forty years. He's a farmer, so it's been difficult for him to hunt long hours in the field. It takes an army of farmers to plant, grow, and harvest the food our nation needs, and Earl has been doing his share of the work. Earl takes off two days a year to put venison in his freezer, so he doesn't have the luxury of being picky. Throughout the years, he's shot several basket bucks and does, but the giants have always managed to elude the reticle of his scope. Until that morning, apparently.

As Earl pulled into my driveway, the only thing brighter than the orange vest he wore was the twinkle in his eyes. He got out of the truck, and together we walked to the bed, leaning over to look inside. Resting on the spare tire was a 1½-year-old 5x5 that would have scored around 110 inches. Earl hit me in the arm, grinned from ear to ear, and then said, "He's a nice one, huh?"

Just five hours later, another friend, Scott, called to tell me that he'd shot a mature buck that afternoon. He was almost hyperventilating on the phone as he described the story. That windy November day had been slow, until that buck chased a doe through the woods in Scott's direction. He pulled up and made a quick, close shot, dropping the buck in his tracks.

Scott ended the story by saying, "I'll text you a photo, Zeke. He's a nice one!"

Two minutes after we finished the call, my phone chimed, and I pulled up a picture of Scott holding a 4½-year-old buck in his hands. His smile reminded me of Earl's smile from a few hours earlier. Later that evening, Scott put the measuring tape on the antlers and totaled up a gross score of 176 inches.

Many things in life are relative. A nice bass to one fisherman isn't necessarily a trophy to another. It's good and appropriate to have relative opinions on what constitutes a "shooter" buck, or who was the best football player of all time, or what is the best truck ever made. Each man's opinion, which depends on his values, experiences, and community, makes his answer valid.

We run into problems, however, when we view truth as relative. This is called "moral relativism," and it suggests that truth and positions of morality are not absolute but relative to each person's belief system. One of the natural consequences of moral relativism is that it becomes impossible for one person to tell another person that something is wrong or right. According to the moral relativist, poaching a trophy buck off of a neighbor's land is not *absolutely* wrong. It's only *possibly* wrong—it all depends on what he deems to be right or wrong.

Christians believe that God defines truth and communicates it to us through his Word. We can know what is right and what is wrong, what is good and what is evil, because our Creator gave us absolute truth. As our heavenly Father, he loves us and desires that we live informed, robust, healthy lives. May we receive his love and walk in his ways, reading the Scriptures and upholding what we know is true.

Prayer

God, help me define right and wrong according to your holy Word. I don't want to be a moral relativist, deciding what I think is right and wrong. You alone are God, and I want to let you determine morality for my life. Amen.

88

THE TROJAN HORSE

Scripture Passage: *"The path of the righteous is like the light of dawn, which shines brighter and brighter until full day. The way of the wicked is like deep darkness; they do not know over what they stumble."* —Proverbs 4:18–19

READ: PSALM 1

Pornography is the Trojan horse of our day. It's attractive to men on the outside, but it ushers in death when it's welcomed into our lives. If you need proof that the enemy of our souls, Satan, takes God's gifts and twists them to deceive us, you'll find no better example than pornography. Satan has perverted God's designs, exploiting women's bodies and feeding men's desires and lusts.

The lie our enemy tells us is that, as long as we keep it secret, engaging with pornography won't hurt the other areas of our lives. I was thirteen when I first viewed a *Playboy* magazine. I was on a duck hunting trip with a friend, his father, and a few other men. One of the adults handed me the magazine and said, "Here you go, Zeke. There's no harm in peeking."

But is there? Does looking at pornography only have an impact on us in the moment we view it? Absolutely not! Pornography objectifies women's bodies, detaching women from their souls, personalities, and relationships. When men engage with pornography, women become sexual objects, merely bodies and body parts. A man once told me that his addiction to pornography changed how he viewed the women in church. He said, "I can't even watch a woman sing on the worship team without picturing her with her clothes off." A culture of pornography is a setting in which women feel insecure and unsafe around men, and men feel ashamed and dirty around the women in their lives.

The approach that friends, spouses, and counselors often take with men involved in pornography is to shame them. This isn't entirely inappropriate, because we should feel ashamed of our sin. However, shame isn't a sufficient long-term motivator. It might cause men to log off their computers for a couple days, but eventually the memory-erasing power of time removes the sense of shame, and they inevitably return to the smut trough for another meal.

It's not enough to motivate with shame; we need to motivate with pleasure. Many men use pornography because they crave more life. They're bored. They feel dead inside, and the brief rush of viewing naked women makes them feel alive. I grew up around pornography. What convinced me to say no was the vision of pleasure that I saw in walking faithfully with God. I realized when I was in my twenties that I had a choice to make: Do I believe that obeying God and walking in his ways will produce more happiness, peace, and contentment than I would find in pornography? The image in Psalm 1—a fruitful tree planted beside streams of water—won me over.

Psalm 1 does not promise that everything in life will go well for someone who chooses Jesus over pornography. What it does promise is the experience of God's nearness, a clean conscience, and a life of productivity. It promises that, over the course of your life, you will experience more soul pleasure and excitement with God than with pornography. The only long-lasting strategy for saying no to pornography is truly believing the promise of God in Psalm 16:11: "You make known to me the path of life; in your presence there is fullness of joy; at your right hand are pleasures forevermore."

*P*rayer

My Father in heaven, please give me faith in you and your pleasures that is powerful enough to make me say no to pornography and lust. I do believe that being faithful to you is the path of life and that you reward faith with "pleasures forevermore." Give me the strength of your Spirit, which is far greater than my temptations to look at things that will destroy me. Amen.

89

SOMETHING'S COMING

Scripture Passage: *"But as it is, they desire a better country, that is, a heavenly one. Therefore God is not ashamed to be called their God, for he has prepared for them a city."* —Hebrews 11:16

READ: REVELATION 21–22

I felt such deep pity for the grizzly bear at the Denver Zoo. She was an eight-hundred-pound sow, and she was resting three feet from the guardrail that held me back—not that I needed a guardrail, mind you. She turned her head as I approached, and our eyes met. I was with a group of friends, and they walked on. I sat on the bench and watched the massive beast for the next twenty minutes to see what she would do. She did nothing. She didn't even move her head. Her eyes stared into mine the entire time, expressing a sense of defeat and misery. I wondered how much more of life she would be experiencing if she was in the wild, in her home.

We also are not at home. We simply weren't made to live in this sin-riddled, fallen world. God has put eternity into each of our hearts, and this causes us to long. The longer we live, the more we yearn for home with an ache in our bones. C. S. Lewis writes, "I must keep alive in myself the desire for my true country, which I shall not find till after death; I must never let it get snowed under or turned aside; I must make it the main object of life to press on to that other country and to help others do the same."[1]

Several years later, during a trip to Alaska, my suspicions about that miserable grizzly in the zoo were confirmed. Over the course of a week, I watched dozens of bears hunt, fish, and range over the berry-rich tundra of America's wildest territory. One afternoon

1. C. S. Lewis, *Mere Christianity* (New York: HarperCollins, 1952), 137.

I had a close encounter with a sow and her cub. At 125 yards, I watched her meander around an open meadow, eating wild bush berries with her cub. Her muscles rippled and rolled. Her coat shined. Her cub rolled around by her feet, occasionally jumping up to taunt Mom. The adult grizzly was alive and thriving, and unlike the bear in the zoo, she didn't have a longing stare. The difference? She was home.

We will be home someday, too. We will no longer experience misery, tragedy, or loneliness. We will be with friends and family in an environment so unspeakably beautiful that Jesus used the word *paradise* to describe it. And in this place of beauty, we will enjoy feasts, adventures, and relationships so rich that we will never long for the places or people we have known before. We will have fresh legs for the unending adventures ahead. This is the Bible's picture of heaven, and it is meant to create a longing for home in our hearts.

Look around you, friend. Everything in creation reminds us that things are not as they should be. Joni Eareckson Tada said, "Can you hear the sighing in the wind? Can you feel the heavy silence in the mountains? Can you sense the restless longing in the sea? Can you see it in the woeful eyes of an animal? Something's coming . . . something better."[2] Something better *is* coming; it's called *home*—and I want you to be there with me.

Prayer

Father, give me the patience and strength of heart to wait for heaven. I love much about this life that you have created, but I long for things to be better . . . to be as you had originally intended for them to be. My heart feels restless for the life you have created me to live. Please help me live well now, as I wait to go home. Amen.

2. Joni Eareckson Tada, quoted in Randy Alcorn, *Heaven* (Wheaton: Tyndale, 2004), 449.

90

A Strong Finish

Scripture Passage: *"And let us not grow weary of doing good, for in due season we will reap, if we do not give up."* —Galatians 6:9

READ: HEBREWS 12:12–17

The most physically challenging hunt I've ever been on was for brown bear in Alaska. The first day of the hunt, a bush pilot flew me in and dropped me off in the middle of the most majestic land I've ever seen. To this day, when people ask me where exactly I hunted in Alaska, I draw a wide circle in the middle of the state map and say, "Someplace in this area."

For eight days I hiked up and down mountains, floated down rivers, and glassed open ravines. I filled the memory cards in my camera on that trip, but not my tag. Still, I had a breakthrough moment on the very last afternoon. I had been cold and tired for seven and a half days, so when we stopped for lunch, I was tempted to take a nap in camp and simply wait for the plane. Then the thought struck me that not finishing strong would be grossly inappropriate. I came to Alaska to hunt hard start to finish, and quitting four hours early would be a decision I'd regret the rest of my life. So, after eating a plate of noodles and a couple of granola bars, I strapped on my pack, chose the largest mountain in our basin, and started for the top.

The author of Hebrews was writing to Christians who had been through horribly difficult challenges. Many had been beaten for their faith in Jesus. Others had been killed. All had been ridiculed for following a man who was crucified as a criminal by the Romans. The temptation to quit and simply shrink into anonymity was powerfully strong among these struggling believers. So in Hebrews 12:12–14, the author gives them a pep talk. He charges them to do two things: press on in strength and integrity, and strive for peace with everyone.

To press on in strength and integrity requires that we dig down deep into the fabric of our faith and choose to obey God with passion and commitment. When the world challenges our commitment to Christ, making fun of us or persecuting us for our beliefs, we power on by God's strength. No compromising to please others; we live for Christ—preaching his truth, obeying his commands, and living out his character and integrity.

The second command is connected to the first: we should aim at having close, honorable relationships. Hebrews 12:14 tell us to "strive for peace with everyone, and for the holiness without which no one will see the Lord." We shouldn't change the gospel message, but we should always try to love others well. Striving for peace means serving, listening, and speaking with gentleness and kindness.

Alaska has a thousand ways to exhaust, challenge, and possibly kill a hunter. Likewise, this world is bent against God and has a thousand ways to make walking with Jesus difficult and exhausting. This should come as no surprise to those of us who love Jesus; our Lord reminds us, "If the world hates you, know that it has hated me before it hated you" (John 15:18). We knew there would be challenges to following Christ when we embarked on this journey. The question isn't, "Will it be difficult to finish well?" It will be difficult, severely difficult. The question for us then is, "Will I find the legs, heart, and faith to finish well in the face of all the struggles and challenges?"

My sincere hope is that someday we will be able to greet one another in heaven and say, "By the grace of God, I finished well . . . and so did you!"

Prayer

My Father, I want to live my life in such a way that, when it's my turn to die, I won't have strong regret. I want to know that I lived well, keeping you my greatest treasure and priority. I need your strength and help on this journey, Father. I pray for my sportsmen brothers who are on this journey with me. Please help them finish well, by your grace. Amen.

Zeke Pipher is the author of *Man on the Run* and is a freelance outdoor writer whose work regularly appears in several magazines, such as *Deer & Deer Hunting*, *Peterson's Bowhunting*, and *Bow & Arrow Hunting*. He speaks on topics such as hunting strategies, the life of a sportsman, marriage, parenting, and priorities.

Pipher is the senior pastor at Heartland Evangelical Free Church in Central City, Nebraska, and earned his MDiv from Talbot School of Theology and his DMin from Gordon-Conwell Theological Seminary. He and his wife, Jamie, have three children and live on an acreage a mile from the Platte River in central Nebraska, where they hike, hunt, fish, camp, and swim.

Keep in touch with sportsman

ZEKE PIPHER

at

zekepipher.com